P9-CEC-788

Throw Like a Girl

*How to Dream Big
and Believe In Yourself*

Jennie Finch with Ann Killion

TRIUMPH
BOOKS

Copyright © 2011 by Jennie Finch

No part of this publication may be reproduced, stored in a retrieval system, or transmitted in any form by any means, electronic, mechanical, photocopying, or otherwise, without the prior written permission of the publisher, Triumph Books, 542 South Dearborn Street, Suite 750, Chicago, Illinois 60605.

Triumph Books and colophon are registered trademarks of Random House, Inc.

Library of Congress Cataloging-in-Publication Data

Finch, Jennie.
  Throw like a girl : how to dream big and believe in yourself / Jennie Finch with Ann Killion.
      p. cm.
  ISBN 978-1-60078-560-3
  1. Softball for women. 2. Self-esteem in women. I. Killion, Ann. II. Title.
  GV881.3.F56 2011
  796.357'8082—dc22

                            2011010286

This book is available in quantity at special discounts for your group or organization. For further information, contact:
  Triumph Books
  542 South Dearborn Street
  Suite 750
  Chicago, Illinois 60605
  (312) 939-3330
  Fax (312) 663-3557
  www.triumphbooks.com

Printed in U.S.A.
ISBN: 978-1-60078-560-3
Design by Patricia Frey
All photos courtesy the Finch family unless otherwise noted.

To my parents, Doug and Beverly, who have always supported me and encouraged me to dream big and believe in myself. And to all the girls who are the true inspiration for this book.

Contents

Acknowledgments
vii

Introduction
xi

Chapter 1
Dream and Believe
1

Chapter 2
Embracing Butterflies and Taking Risks
15

Chapter 3
Getting Fit: Some Basics
27

Chapter 4
Accepting Who You Are: Body Image, Dieting, and Nutrition
41

II. MIND

Chapter 5
Busting Stereotypes: Why Are People Always Trying to Label Us?
53

Chapter 6
The High Wire Act: How to Keep Your Balance
65

Chapter 7

What's the Payoff? Where Will Sports Get Me?

79

Chapter 8

The Pressure Cooker: Handling Pressure from Parents, Adults, and Peers

93

Chapter 9

Mental Preparation: Your Mind Is Your Most Important Muscle

107

Chapter 10

The Team: Leadership, Great Teammates, and Not So Great

121

Chapter 11

Inspiration: Where to Find It, How to Tap Into It

135

Chapter 12

Pressure as a Positive: Embrace the Heat

151

Chapter 13

Being a Role Model: Accepting the Big Responsibility

173

Chapter 14

Winning and Losing

187

Chapter 15

The Gold Medal

203

Acknowledgments

FROM JENNIE:

For my entire life, I've been blessed with a large, incredible support system. This book, and whatever else I've accomplished in life, is thanks to those wonderful people who I've leaned on for advice, guidance, and love.

So a heartfelt thank you to:

Casey, Ace, and Diesel—You fill my heart with such joy daily. I only wish I could express all that you have brought to my life. I am eternally grateful.

My parents—You are both my backbone. Dad, you have always given me unconditional love, confidence, dreams, motivation; you have always urged me to do what is right. You are the best coach I've ever had! Mom, you are my rock—always there for me, always ready with a hug, and always knowing just what I need at just the right time. Thank you both for your support, your sacrifices, and your love.

Shane and Landon—You are such wonderful big brothers and terrific roles models. Thank you for toughening me up, lighting my competitive fire, inspiring me, and for your friendship and love.

My extended family—My grandparents who have always been my biggest fans and spiritual lights. My nieces and nephews who inspire me daily. My in-laws, the Daigles—thank you for accepting me and embracing the crazy lives that Casey and I have lived and for making me feel so at home with you. Thank you for allowing and encouraging our dreams. Thanks for all you have sacrificed and the many opportunities you have given us and most of all for your love!

The Bomb Squad—The four of you have been my best friends since high school, my accountability sisters, my go-to gang. You have shown me what cool really is. Thank you for inspiring me and loving me unconditionally.

Toni—my best friend, my fellow warrior. Thank you for creating so many memories and laughs.

All my incredible amazing teammates who have inspired me— There are too many to name! You are the sisters I never had. You pushed me, motivated me, helped me become a better person and player. I could never thank you all enough! There is no "I" in team, and it always has been and will be "we!"

My Wildcat family—What a wonderful, life-changing, life-lasting experience I had at U of A! My biggest thanks goes to Coach Candrea—you helped my dreams come true on and off the field with your guidance, support, and love.

Erin Kane—for all your support and guidance and friendship. Thank you for making things happen and all you do daily! Most importantly believing in Women in Sport and representing us so well!

The JFSCamp Crew—I couldn't do it without you.

My USA Softball family. I've been so blessed to represent the greatest country and travel the world with you all! Thank you for the incredible honor and many memories all over the world!

The USOC.

NPF and the Chicago Bandits. Thank you for the chance to play professionally! Bill Sokolis—your ownership, dedication, sacrifice that allowed and provided the "pro" opportunity.

Mizuno and all of my sponsors.

To my fans and supporters. You are my daily inspiration!

And to my main inspiration, my Lord and Savior Jesus Christ, my light and salvation. All glory be given to You!

Acknowledgments

A special thanks to the women who came before me, paving the way, breaking down barriers, and shining the light. And to the young women and girls who are the future of not only sports, but society. The future is bright because of you!

Ann Killion—Thank you for stepping up to the plate and swinging away! Thanks for making this dream come true. Thank you for being so easy to work with and bringing in your incredible experience and talent to this project. Thank you for your dedication and superb coverage of Women in Sport and paving the way for female sportswriters!

FROM ANN KILLION:

To my family: My daughter, Kaitlin, for your inspiration, your proofreading, and input, and your spirit and dedication on the court and the field. My son, Connor, for your support and humor and for once asking when you were very small, "Mommy, can boys be sportswriters?" My husband, Matt, for your patience and support and your dedication to coaching girls and encouraging them to be their best, on and off the court.

To Farley Chase for your guidance, to Joan Ryan for your recommendation and advice.

To Karen O'Brien and the others at Triumph Books for their skill and expertise.

And to all the inspiring women athletes who have shared their stories with me over the years—you've changed the world, forever.

Introduction

When I look at the course of my life, I wonder where I would be without sports? And I don't just mean how I would have spent my time. *Who* would I be?

Certainly someone very different. Because softball has not only blessed me with wonderful opportunities and experiences, it has shaped the very core of who I am. Sports has helped mold my confidence, my values, my friendships, my self-esteem, my interactions with others, my goals, my work ethic—everything about my life!

The life lessons that I learned through playing sports apply to so many parts of my life. Every day I draw on them and am thankful for my experience. That's why I wanted to write this book: to impart some of those lessons, and to encourage girls and young women to play, to have fun, and to dream big.

I wanted to write a book that spoke to what I have so often been concerned about and wondered about; a book that could inspire, motivate, and inform. When I was young I used to devour any magazines or books that had any information about girls and sports; unfortunately, there weren't many resources out there. There still aren't.

Yet I see thousands of young girls every year through my camps and other appearances. And I see the light shining in their eyes—the same excitement that I used to feel when I stepped onto the softball field.

They are engaged and enthusiastic and looking for information. And there are millions more like them.

But when I look around the mainstream sports world, there's a disconnect. Those girls don't have the same nurturing, encouragement, and support systems that young boys can easily access. They're looking for different information, unique to females.

For years, I've heard girls express their concerns: questions about coaches, colleges, teammates, motivation, balance. I want to assure them that conflict with a coach or a bad experience with a teammate or an overloaded schedule is not the end of the world.

In addition, my work with the Women's Sports Foundation and other groups has given me a window on the issues that so many girls are grappling with on a daily basis. I hope that girls and the adults who love and support them will find this book to be a resource in both inspirational and practical ways. Though I played softball, this isn't a book just for softball players or hardcore athletes. This is book for all girls who are not only interested in sports and fitness but also want to connect with the values and lessons sports can teach.

Girls are beautiful, multi-faceted, dynamic creatures. My goal has been to speak to the whole girl, which is why the book has been separated into sections called Body, Mind, and Heart. The values and lessons discussed in the following pages address all parts of a girls' life.

It wasn't that long ago that I was an adolescent myself, feeling awkward, pressured, and uncertain. I still feel that way plenty of times! I hope that by sharing my story and the lessons I've learned I can encourage and inspire others to dream and believe.

I. BODY

Chapter 1

Dream and Believe

The assessment was delivered in one cold short sentence: "Jennie's not a championship pitcher."

With that, my softball coach slammed the door on my dreams. On my self-image. On my future. He told my father in no uncertain terms that I was not a winner. Not a champion.

I was 12 years old.

That could have been the end of my story right there. It would make for a very short book—a pamphlet really—titled *Not a Champion* by Jennie Finch. That's what would have happened if I allowed someone else to define me. If I accepted someone else's limits on myself. If I let another person tell me who I was, rather than listen to my own dreams.

Instead, I chose to believe in myself.

FALLING IN LOVE WITH SPORTS

My father, Doug, believed in me, too. He had seen me fall in love with the game of softball, growing and learning, eager for bigger challenges. He had seen me battle as hard as any boy—and with two older sons he had worked with plenty of boys and young men. He knew that I was tough and strong.

He knew that I could be a champion.

I started playing softball when I was five. My parents first noticed that I had a strong arm when we were spending Christmas with my grandparents in Iowa. A California kid, I was thrilled by the snow. I packed a snowball and tossed it so far that no one saw where it landed. Mom and Dad looked at each other—how did their little girl get such an arm?

Whether it was heaving snowballs or softballs, I loved to throw and catch. In our family, we were avid fans of the Los Angeles Dodgers, who played not far from our home in La Mirada, California. Mom was actually the biggest fan, sharing season tickets with friends at work. She used to take my brothers and me to games. When the Dodgers won the World Series in 1988, we were all thrilled. My dream was to play for the Dodgers—I didn't know any better.

While my dreams of playing Major League Baseball were far off in the future, my present was filled with softball. I loved the game. I loved hitting, fielding, sweating, getting dirty, working in the batting cage, being with teammates. And most of all I loved pitching. I loved having the ball in my hand at the start of every play when my team was in the field. I loved being involved.

Pretty soon my parents started getting advice from people in the softball world. They saw I had some talent and suggested I should

> *"Champions keep playing until they get it right."*
> —Billie Jean King, tennis player and women's sports advocate

spread my wings and find a more competitive league. Some people in our community thought I should stay in La Mirada. For me, that was the start of learning about politics in sports. My parents wanted to do what was best for me, and they were teaching me that I should strive to be the best I can be. But sometimes that means going against what everyone else is doing.

Eventually, I joined a powerhouse travel ball team called the Firecrackers. It was such a big deal to make that team. And they had invited me for a tryout—they wanted me! I was so proud.

I was one of the younger players. Most of the girls were a year older than me. They were physically more mature than I was, and they had all played together for a few years. I felt naïve and intimidated, like an outsider trying to break into their little clique. I worked hard to overcome my shyness and tried to make friends with my new teammates and fit in to this dominating team.

But every time my turn would come up to pitch in a tournament championship game, the coach always found an excuse not to pitch me. Over and over again, he'd pitch his daughter or some other girl. But never me.

Finally, my father asked him why. After all, I was playing really well. We were a dedicated family. I never missed practice. Why couldn't I ever get the chance?

"Because," the coach told my father, "Jennie's not a championship pitcher."

When I heard that, I was devastated. Did he see something in me that I couldn't see? Was he right?

The self-doubt flooded in. We later learned that the team hadn't really wanted me—they had just invited me to join their team so that I wouldn't be on a competing squad. That made me feel even worse.

I loved everything about softball, including hitting. I took pride in being a complete player.

But my father sat me down and said that we were going to make a change. He firmly believed I could pitch in championship games. He'd had enough of youth sports' politics. Though he was an advocate of finishing what you start, he was a bigger advocate of doing what was right for his children. So we left the Firecrackers and started looking for another team.

As with so many tough times in my life, that instance taught me a life lesson. Having to leave my big-time team was an early education that life isn't always fair. It doesn't always go the way you want. But you control what you can. We might not have been able to change one coach's mind, but we could find another team where I wouldn't be prejudged and where I would get a chance.

I dreaded the process. I had to be the new girl all over again. That was a really big deal on a travel ball team because you spent the whole weekend with your team. It was more fun if you had friends to share the experience, and sometimes girls could be mean to the newcomer.

It was awkward being brand new. Again.

LESSONS FROM A DARK FIELD IN THE MIDDLE OF NOWHERE

My new team, the Batbusters, was a better fit right from the start. The girls were friendlier. I was more comfortable.

We were an underdog team. In fact, we didn't qualify for nationals until the very last chance. We had to keep going to different tournaments, trying to qualify. We finally did and went to the ASA (American Softball Association) national championships, which were held in Tennessee.

We advanced to the semifinals in the loser's bracket. Because we had lost once, we couldn't lose again.

And what team was standing in the way of our team and the national championship game? My old team, the Firecrackers—and the same coach who was absolutely sure I couldn't be a championship pitcher.

I dreaded facing them. All spring and summer, every time I saw that team in a tournament, I got a stomachache. I avoided being around the Firecrackers. When I saw them at the opening ceremonies of the nationals—and saw the coach—I remembered what he had said about me. He didn't believe in me. He thought I wasn't a winner.

This game was my chance to prove him wrong. Or if I struggled, I would prove him right. It was up to me.

The game was played late on a hot muggy night on a really dark field out in the Tennessee countryside. I was in the bullpen warming up with my dad. It was almost pitch black out there. I had a blister on my finger that was bleeding and hurting. I was tired. I was scared. I didn't want to pitch.

"I can't go, Dad," I said. "I can't do it."

"Yes you can, Jennie," he said. "You can do this."

My coach came out to see how I was doing. I wanted to tell him, "Coach, someone else will have to pitch." But my dad just said, "She's going. She's ready."

I was shaking as I walked toward the mound on that field in the middle of nowhere. My stomach hurt. I had to pass directly in front of my old team—I could feel all of their eyes staring at me. I had to

*"A great pleasure in life is doing
what people say you cannot do."*
—Walter Bagehot, author

walk right past my old coach who was in the third-base coaching box.
I felt as though he could see the self-doubt seeping out of me. I felt so
nervous. So scared.

But then I stepped into the circle—and the adrenaline kicked in.
All my hard work and training and preparation rose to the surface. I
threw a few pitches. I got the first couple of batters out. I was focused. I
was prepared. I was okay.

My dark cloud of fear lifted. I stopped worrying about the other team
and the coach and whatever they thought of me. The big scary obstacle I
had built up in my mind was gone. I was just a pitcher doing my job.

Back in the bullpen when I had been a scared young girl, my dad
had been very firm. He wasn't being mean—he was showing his belief
in me. Without him, I would have given up. I would have used the
little blister on my finger as an excuse and missed my chance to prove
myself. Dad didn't let me.

When I was little and my father taught me how to ride a bike, he
would run alongside me and push me with his hand. He would be
pushing, pushing, and then all of a sudden I would glance back and he
wasn't pushing me anymore. I was riding my bike without him.

That's what happened that night in Tennessee. He kept pushing
me along, pushing me toward the mound. Without him pushing me
and encouraging me, I would have stayed in my comfort zone. I never
would have stepped up to the challenge. I never would have found out I
could do it on my own.

But I did.

I don't remember the final score of that game, but we won. We sent
my old team back to California, and we went on to the championship
game.

That night, I learned I was strong. I gained an inner confidence that I could continue to draw upon in tough times.

AN ONGOING PROCESS

So that's it, right? I learned that I was a championship pitcher and went on to great things and a wonderful career.

I did. But it's not quite that simple. Life is an ongoing process of learning to be strong, of battling doubts. There's never a moment where you think, *Gosh, I have this all figured out.* I have spent a lifetime trying to prove myself, figuring out who I am, and finding inner strength and self-confidence.

Playing sports helped me do that in so many ways, which is why I wanted to write this book—to share my stories and, hopefully, to provide some motivation and inspiration. Because I'm just like you— I'm working hard everyday to become a better person.

In this book, I hope to share some practical information, things that I wish I'd known growing up or that I found helpful in some of my struggles. I have some advice, tips, and strategies that have helped me. And I want to share with you my inspirations, my hopes and dreams, my struggles and challenges. Because while we are all unique and different, my journey isn't much different from any other girl's.

Through sports I learned to accept and appreciate my body and to accept myself for who I am. I gained confidence and inspiration. Athletics is not only good for your body, it's great for your mind and spirit. And I learned that life is about so much more than just the wins and losses at the end of a game.

"Remember that not getting what you want is sometimes a wonderful stroke of luck."
—Dalai Lama, Tibetan spiritual leader

I feel so privileged to be able to share my experiences with girls at my softball camps.

My expertise is in sports. But the lessons I've learned help me in life: working hard, trying your best, handling pressure, and rising to challenges. These lessons can be applied no matter what passion drives you.

WHY I PLAY

Sometimes I've been asked why I play softball and why I devoted so much of my life to a sport. It's a hard question to answer because the answer is so multi-faceted.

So here are just a few reasons I play:

- I love the game.
- I love the feeling of being part of the team, of playing for the name on the front of my jersey and not the back.

- I love to compete against others and test myself.
- I love to take risks and accept a challenge.
- Because I can! My mother and grandmother never had the opportunity that I have.
- I love to push my body as hard as I can and feel the sweat drip off my face.
- I want to make my family proud of me.
- I love the process and the feeling of satisfaction that comes from working toward goals, both individual and collective.
- Playing helps me both build confidence and overcome the fear of failure.

My sport has given me so much in my life—confidence, a career, a chance to travel the world, great friends, even my husband and children.

I started out as just a little girl with big dreams, some of which weren't very realistic. But I kept dreaming and kept working. I kept nurturing my dreams with the help of my family. I practiced and prepared so that—despite nerves or fears—I was ready for the challenges.

When people lavish me with praise or assume I have it all figured out, I almost have to laugh because inside I feel like I'm still proving

"A true champion is someone who wants to make a difference, who never gives up, and who gives everything she has no matter what the circumstances are. A true champion works hard and never loses sight of her dreams."
—Dot Richardson, softball legend and Hall of Famer

My Inspiration

I feel so privileged to be able to touch the lives of girls around the country and share my own stories of challenges and inspirations. I often hear from girls and their parents who want to tell me their own stories.

Here is a (modified for privacy) letter I received not too long ago that truly touched my heart. I am sharing it with you so you know that whatever is happening in your life you are not alone.

Dear Jennie,

My daughter recently had the pleasure of meeting you at one of your appearances. It was a dream come true for her. I would like to share her story with you.

My daughter was just an average player in her early years. She decided to try pitching when she was 11. She was pretty wild and wasn't one of the Little League stars, so she got very little help and attention. But she always had determination, and she wanted to be just like you someday.

Finally, an older man who had taught his daughters to pitch noticed her, helped her, and got her on target. At 12 she joined a travel team and just blossomed, surpassing other pitchers. She became the starting pitcher on her high school team through a lot of hard work and determination.

Of course it came with some jealousy and controversy, and she lost some friends to jealousy. She sacrificed a lot of teenage activities to practice and had to deal with a lot of stress as a pitcher. I am so proud of her, as she always remained the bigger person in all of the situations she had to face.

Sadly, this last August, her father—who has been ill—started really getting on her about her pitching. In one game, her team lost by one run and her father was out of control. She cried on the mound for the first time in her life and wanted to quit the game. We subsequently had a lot of family turmoil, and my daughter blamed herself. She wanted to quit pitching because of it. Eventually, her father got some help and is doing much better and explained to my daughter that none of this was her fault.

The words you spoke at your appearance went straight to my daughter's heart. As a teenager, sometimes the road seems so rough and lonely. She has looked up to you her whole life. She is determined to continue her pitching, working hard no matter what anyone says, and is ready to face the world.

She has been attending several college showcases and college clinics. With each one, she is gaining faith in herself and gaining excitement at being noticed. She is looking forward to playing this game for many years to come. Thanks for being a positive role model for my daughter both on and off the field. I have been a first grade teacher for 22 years and I know the impact adults can have on children. I just want you to know the difference you have made in my daughter's life and thank you personally for it!

Sincerely and God Bless,
A loving mother

myself. I still feel like that little girl who was told she couldn't be a championship pitcher.

To this day, what that coach said about me echoes in my mind. I continued to see him for years after that night in Tennessee, because I played against his daughter through high school and in college. Never once did I see him without thinking that he never believed I could be a championship pitcher.

In a way, that coach did me a tremendous favor. My experience with him taught me a very valuable lesson: Don't let others determine who you are going to be. In that instance, it was a coach who didn't believe in me. But it could be a boy who doesn't think girls can be strong, or girls at school who are pressuring you to conform, or a science teacher who doesn't think you're smart enough.

There is tremendous power in words. A coach's discouraging words can haunt a kid forever. Every day, I get emails from girls who are thinking of quitting because someone doesn't believe in them. Or I receive letters from parents who want me to give their daughters a few words of encouragement to keep them on track.

Girls today are subjected even more to the power of words, to constant judgment and evaluation. Because of texting and Facebook and the immediacy of communication, we're all exposed to the power of others' words 24 hours a day. It's hard to shut the bedroom door and escape from it all, the way I could when I was a girl. The best defense is a strong belief in yourself and an acceptance of who you are and your individual strengths and talents.

Be you!

This is your life. You only get one. This isn't a practice run for the real thing. You can lead your life the way other people think you should. Or you can follow your own passions and interests. You can lead your life the way *you* believe is best.

I work with so many girls across the country in my camps and clinics. They're all different—sizes, shapes, smiles, personalities—and they're all beautiful. Sometimes I see that they lack confidence or are discouraged. I see how an uncomfortable situation or a disparaging comment can easily push a girl off track and away from her dreams.

Looking back, I realize how many times my path could have gone a different way. I could have faltered or given in to self-doubt. I could have quit and changed my life irrevocably.

That night in Tennessee, I learned to face my fears and fight through them. I learned to rely on my ability—an ability that was honed through preparation and practice. Even though I wasn't confident out in the bullpen, I was ready for that moment.

I learned not to let someone else's opinion or judgment determine who I would be. Through that experience—one that I had dreaded so much—I gained a new layer of confidence, a core of inner strength.

Through the years, I kept building that confidence, adding layers to it. Though I still always feel the fear of failure, I've had enough moments of success that I can draw upon that reservoir of confidence in tough times. That experience enables me to keep going, to keep fighting.

The girl who wasn't supposed to be a championship pitcher won quite a few championship games with her travel ball team.

And won a collegiate national championship at Arizona.

And won a gold medal in Athens, Greece.

And, most importantly, learned that the true measure of a champion is on the inside.

If you dream big and believe in yourself, you never know where you'll end up.

Chapter 2

Embracing Butterflies and Taking Risks

I was five years old when I first trotted out to the T-ball field, missing a tooth and with my hair in a high ponytail. I had no idea I was starting an adventure that would direct the course of my life.

How could I know such a thing? I was just a kid who wanted to have fun, who wanted to be like my brothers and swing a bat. Sometimes I wonder: *What if I hadn't wanted to play?* How different would my life be if I had been too scared to try something new?

You know what? It's impossible for me to even imagine what my life would be like without softball. My sport has given me so much: my most cherished experiences, a chance to see the world, my closest

I didn't know then that softball would shape the course of my life.

friends, and even my wonderful husband. It's opened up so many doors. Because of softball, I've had the chance to meet new people and do things I never dreamed of doing.

My sport helped shape who I am today. It helped me build a core of inner confidence that helps me not only on the field, but in every aspect of my life. I'm still trying to learn and grow and be the best person I can be. And the strength I gained from my sport has helped me every step of the way.

After I finished playing in college, thanks to softball, I suddenly had so many awesome opportunities. For example, ESPN asked me to do commentary on the College Softball World Series. I was so flattered.

And it sounds pretty simple, right? I know softball inside and out. I know most of the girls in the game. I know how to talk. What could be so hard?

Plenty. Like so much in life, this was a huge challenge. Just like playing in a national championship game or in the Olympics, it was nerve-wracking and scary. The reality was I cried myself to sleep in my hotel room every night. I was so nervous before every televised game that I felt physically sick.

Do you ever get that way before a big test or a big game? Or when you have to do something you've never done before? My stomach hurt. I felt like I couldn't breathe. I was convinced that I didn't know what I was doing, that I was unprepared. Every time the camera went on, I had terrible butterflies. I felt like a disaster.

When I was a communications major in college, I enrolled in a public speaking class. I don't know what I expected—maybe that we would just learn in theory how to speak in public, but not actually have to do it! On the first day, when I found out that we had to give three speeches in front of the entire class, I transferred out—there was no way I was going to make those speeches! Standing in the pitcher's circle in front of thousands of screaming fans was easy for me. Standing up in front of people and speaking? No way.

But when I started working with ESPN, I sure wished I hadn't dropped that class. Because just like sports—and so many things in life—learning to speak in public or on television requires practice and a lot of preparation.

I was very fortunate to have really talented people helping me. They were like having a great coach. I took all the advice I could from the experts. I practiced. I studied. I did as much prep work as I could.

Fast-forward a few years, and now I'm much more comfortable doing television. I still get nervous and feel the butterflies, but I enjoy the work. I'm honored to be asked to provide commentary on my sport or to give speeches or to be on discussion panels.

But before I could get to that point, I had to take a risk. I had to plunge in. If I had simply stayed in my comfort zone, I would have

Gaining the confidence to speak in public required practice and preparation—just like sports.

turned down all those great opportunities. I wouldn't have learned how to do television or have had other career doors open for me.

It's the same with anything in life. It's the same with sports or any new activity. I recommend getting out of your comfort zone and plunging in.

That's what I encourage you to do with sports—and in life. Go for it!

MAKING IT A "WANT TO"

You don't need me to tell you that activity and exercise are important. Every time you turn on a TV or pick up a magazine you hear that message.

The reasons are abundant. Obesity is on the rise in our country, creating health issues and shortening lives. Regular exercise is shown to prevent disease, create happier lives, increase a girl's self-esteem, and decrease her risk of pregnancy and drug abuse. Sports participation can be empowering and is linked to academic success, leadership, and overall confidence in young women. The list of all the good things that exercise and sports participation can bring goes on and on.

But you probably have a lot of other lists in your life:

You've got to do your homework, get good grades, look good, hang out with your friends, and be a good daughter. The last thing you need is another "have to" on your list.

So I hope you can turn sports and exercise into a "want to."

Why?

Because it is *so much fun*! And once you start, you feel so much stronger and so empowered.

I was lucky. I was just a little kid when I found my sport and unlocked my passion. Growing up in Southern California, sports were always part of our family's life. I have two older brothers, Shane and Landon, who played basketball and baseball. We were a baseball-crazy family. We loved the Los Angeles Dodgers so much that one year we even turned our Christmas card into a tribute to the team.

So when I came along, my parents didn't think twice about enrolling me in sports. My dad put a glove on my hand and tossed me a ball. At the age of five, I was introduced to softball.

And I loved it. I liked the uniform. I liked being on a team. I liked that it was something that I did that was different from my brothers. I liked being outside on the green grass. I liked the punch and snacks afterward.

"Life is like riding a bicycle. To keep your balance you must keep moving."
—Albert Einstein, scientist

We were crazy about the Dodgers. Their World Series victory inspired that year's Finch Christmas card.

It wasn't as though I landed on this planet already formed as a great softball player. It was an evolution. When I was about seven the coach wanted to see who could throw the ball to home plate. If you could, then you'd get to pitch. I was bigger than most of my teammates, so I could get the ball that far. And that's how I started my pitching career—by lining up and throwing the ball to home plate. Not exactly a show of overwhelming talent.

But I took it from there. I had found my niche. I wasn't the coolest girl. I wasn't the prettiest girl. I wasn't the most popular. I was too tall. I was chunky. I was bigger than most of the boys.

The *Real* Benefits of Sports and Exercise

I'm proud to be a member of the Women's Sports Foundation. It's an influential organization founded by Billie Jean King, the legendary tennis player. During the past few decades, the Women's Sports Foundation has become a very important resource for girls in sports. One of the great things the WSF does is conduct research on the benefits of sports.

Here are just a few of the findings of WSF's 2009 report "Her Life Depends on It: Sport, Physical Activity, and the Health and Well-Being of American Girls and Women."

- Educational gains: Girls who participated in high school sports were more likely to complete college than those who did not participate in sports.
- Smoking: Girls who participated on one or two school or community sports teams were significantly less likely to smoke regularly than non-athletes.
- Illicit drug use: Two nationwide studies found that girls who played on school or community sports teams were significantly less likely to use illegal drugs.
- Depression: Moderate levels of exercise and/or sports activity helped protect girls against depression.
- Breast cancer risk: studies found that women who had the highest physical activity during adolescence and young adulthood were 20 percent less likely to get breast cancer later in life.
- Osteoporosis: Studies found that young girls who exercise regularly can increase their bone mass, thus protecting them against the onset of osteoporosis later in life.

If you want more information, go to www.womensportsfoundation.org.

But through athletics, I found a way to fit in. I was the first girl picked when we were choosing sides for kickball teams in elementary school. I couldn't wait for the softball throw we did once a year as part of our Junior Olympics program—because I won it every year. I liked being called "sporty" or a "jock." I had found something that clicked inside of me.

I was lucky. I found my passion early, and I stuck with it. Even through the hard times—when I was stressed out or felt pressure or was mad at my dad for pushing me—the good parts of my sport kept me going.

You also may have found your favorite sport or favorite activity early in life. But you may not have. Or you might want to try something else. Or you might not think sports and exercise are for you.

If you belong to the last group, I hope I can change your mind. Even getting out for a walk every day is important. Getting your muscles moving, your heart pumping, your lungs filling with air is important. Those muscles, that heart, those lungs—they belong to you for the rest of your life. You wouldn't think about not brushing your hair or your teeth. But you've got to take care of the rest of yourself, too.

Plus, it feels great. There's a secret little ingredient called endorphins—natural chemicals that are released in your body when you exercise. And they make you feel happier. They relieve stress. They chase away depression.

After even a little bit of exercise, some of the things that were stressing you out earlier in the day don't seem so important or menacing. A workout can be like a little vacation for your body and your mind.

If you haven't found an activity that feels right for you, you might feel shy or uncomfortable about trying something new.

Here's my best advice on that: Take a risk! And keep searching until you find something you love.

GOING FOR IT

Don't worry if other girls have been doing a sport for years. Don't worry about whether you're good enough to make high school varsity, or travel team, or get a college scholarship. Don't worry about making a mistake.

We've all been beginners at some point. When I was in high school, I already had a reputation for being a pretty good softball player. But I wanted to try playing basketball and volleyball, too.

I could have been concerned about being awkward and potentially embarrassed or not being the best. Those girls I was playing against had been playing their particular sports since they were five, just the way I had been playing softball. But I decided: who cares? Who cares if I'm not the best or if I make mistakes? If I worry about that, I'll never try anything new. At 14 I was a little too young to stop trying new things!

I decided I couldn't be so worried about what other people think. And I would hate to miss out on something that could be so fun just because I was feeling insecure. It turns out that playing those other two sports was a total blast and something that I think really helped me in softball. I became more aware of my body, more agile. I had the experience of playing a sport just for fun without a lot of the background pressures of a travel team or scholarships.

If I had never tried playing those other sports, I would totally regret it to this day.

Life is all about taking risks. I get really bad butterflies—even now. But in a way I embrace those butterflies because they let me know I'm out of my comfort zone. My butterflies tell me that I'm alive, trying

"Take chances, make mistakes. That's how you grow. Pain nourishes your courage. You have to fail in order to practice being brave."
—Mary Tyler Moore, actress

new things, testing myself. I always try to take that nervous energy and use it in a productive way. My teammates can tell when I have my game face on—I get pretty focused. My butterflies help me do that.

The only way you can get out of your comfort zone is to take a risk, to try something you're not sure you can do, to challenge yourself. Otherwise life is just one big helping of sameness. If we don't step out of our comfort zone, we're never going to go anywhere new.

I run softball camps and clinics for girls all around the country. I see girls of all different ages and all different levels of ability. Sure, natural talent plays a role in some players' aptitude for the game. But I find that enthusiasm, hard work, and a good attitude are the most important ingredients to success. Talent, in truth, will only get you so far.

That's why I always tell my campers, why be good when you can be great? You can be good with talent. But what it takes for greatness is a little extra effort and a lot of preparation.

If you're already involved in a sport, congratulations and keep going for it! If you're not, you might be wondering how to get started.

HOW TO GET STARTED

There are a lot of ways to get started with a fitness and sports program. It can be as basic as going for a jog with your dog. Or taking a walk around the block listening to your favorite music. Or getting some of your trusted friends to go out and throw the ball around with you, shoot hoops at the local basketball court, or strap on a pair of roller skates.

Your city's Parks and Recreation department is a great resource; they probably have leagues at all different levels. There are summer camps that are either sports-specific or teach basic skills for several different sports. Your physical education teachers are also helpful resources. And school sports are a terrific place to start—most coaches expect that some of their players won't be expert athletes. The freshman and JV teams are

"What do you first do when you learn how to swim?
You make mistakes.... And what happens?
You make other mistakes, and when you have
made all the mistakes you possibly can without
drowning what do you find? That you can swim.
Well, life is just the same as learning to swim.
Do not be afraid of making mistakes, for there is
no other way of learning how to live."
–Alfred Adler, physician

places to learn how to play sports. And there's nothing more fun than representing your school!

If you're in college and want to join a team, intramurals and club teams are great. Sometimes dorms and sororities have their own teams, too.

And if you don't feel like a team sport is for you, jump in the pool, put on your running shoes, or get out your yoga mat. There isn't one formula for staying active and healthy. Just find what works for you.

And most of all—have fun!

Jennie's Tips on Finding the Right Sport for You

1. Decide if you want to play an individual sport or a team sport. You might feel less peer pressure in an individual sport. But you also might miss out on the camaraderie of a team, which can make sports so much fun. Sports like track, cross-country, or swimming can allow the best of both worlds.

2. Decide if you want to play with your friends, and join their team. If they have more experience than you do, ask them for pointers and advice.

3. Check out your local recreation department to see what they offer in the way of teams, lessons, or camps.

4. Practice on your own to gain confidence and get your body used to the moves you need for your sport.

5. Just get started! There's never a perfect moment. Don't procrastinate!

Chapter 3

Getting Fit:
Some Basics

My dad was my pitching coach. He was—and is—my biggest fan. And, luckily for me, he was also my drill sergeant, motivator, and alarm clock.

Though we often butted heads about practice, I was lucky to have him there to keep me on schedule with my fitness and my pitching. Sometimes I wonder if I could have ever developed the same work ethic without him. He never let me slide.

"There's only one way to do something, and that's the right way," my dad was famous for saying.

That's hard to hear sometimes, especially when you're a teenager and you feel like you have so much pressure to do *everything* the right way.

But that was how I approached my sport and workouts and my life. I tried to do it the right way. I tried to give 100 percent all the time.

The hardest thing in fitness is just getting started. Everyone has good intentions, but good intentions while you're sitting on the couch watching *Project Runway* or updating your status on Facebook don't create results.

The only worthwhile good intentions are the ones you act on.

If you're an athlete already, with a regular routine that you stick to religiously, never ever slacking off, you can jump ahead.

But if you ever need a little motivation to get going—and let's face it, who doesn't?—then keep reading.

MENTAL DOS AND DON'TS

Remember that a huge part of physical fitness is mental. I've found that it helps me so much to have the right mindset: a game plan, a strategy. If I don't have the right mental attitude I'm pretty sure that I'm not going to make the right progress physically.

How do you get that right mindset?

DO: Carve out time for your workout. If you don't actually schedule it into your busy day, you will almost always come up with an excuse for not doing it. Making it part of your regular routine is the best approach. Even write it down in your planner, along with your homework assignments.

DO: Find a time that works best for you. I've found that if I don't exercise in the morning, when I'm at my best, I don't get as good of a workout. I also might end up sacrificing my workout because of other unpredictable things in my day—and then I'm only cheating myself.

"Mental will is a muscle that needs exercise, just like the muscles of the body."
—Lynn Jennings, distance runner

Find time to schedule your workouts and make them fun! (AP Images)

DON'T: Bite off more than you can chew. One of the big mistakes a lot of people make is jumping into an exercise plan, going full throttle for a couple of days, and then giving up because their muscles are sore or it took too much time or it was harder than they expected.

If your expectations are unrealistic, your body is going to have a hard time matching them. I try to be realistic in my goals.

DO: Make it enjoyable. Pick an activity you like. If you don't like running, then walk or ride a bike or roller skate. Find a friend to work out with. Listen to your favorite music while you're exercising. When you hit a workout goal, reward yourself with a treat—not necessarily food, but your favorite nail polish or those new jeans you've been wanting.

DON'T: Come up with excuses. Treat your workout like something that's not optional—like a homework assignment or brushing your teeth. I find that if I put on my workout clothes, I'm halfway there. Make it part of your daily routine.

FITNESS BASICS

There are three main components of exercise: aerobic, strength training, and flexibility training. We need all three to be truly fit.

Aerobic

Find something fun!

The aerobic part of fitness is usually the first step. Find a way to get your heart rate up and get a sweat going. Aerobic workouts are the foundation for physical fitness, no matter what kind of sport you're doing. Even though I was a pitcher, I had to get my running in. It was mandatory for my overall fitness: my stamina, endurance, and recovery time.

I'm a big fan of interval training: pushing myself to the maximum for short bursts and interspersing those bursts with lower intensity activity, like walking or jogging. Interval training is great for building endurance and for developing fast twitch muscles.

There are so many ways to get a good aerobic workout: brisk walking or hiking, running, biking (road or stationary), basketball, soccer, swimming. Find something you like and stick with it, or mix it up by doing different activities on different days. That's called cross-training.

If you're just beginning, I think it's wise to start out with manageable chunks of time, such as 15 or 20 minutes, and work up from there. If you are already working out regularly, push yourself a little more. See if you can run a little faster or a little longer. Try to push yourself every day.

Strength
Don't be intimidated!

Strength training—building muscle through weight training—is something I didn't take up until college. And to be honest, I get concerned with too much weight training in younger girls. I see kids who use improper techniques or who are getting too loaded up on weights—and all that will do is lead to injuries. When your body is growing, you need to be careful not to overload it and put too much stress on your frame and your growth plates.

When I first got to the University of Arizona, I started hitting the weight room. They gave me the "Barbie bar"—the lightest bar in the gym—to lift. It was about 40 pounds, lighter than what most of my teammates were lifting. But when I started lifting, my legs began shaking. I thought, *Wow, I have a really long way to go.*

> *"Those who think they have no time for bodily exercise will sooner or later have to find time for illness."*
> —Edward Stanley, British Prime Minister

I was so sore from lifting weights my freshman year—and so hungry all the time! Here I thought I'd been in such great shape from playing so many sports in high school and playing travel ball all the time, and it turned out I wasn't nearly as prepared for the next level as I thought I was.

That was a big lesson. When I came back for my sophomore year, I brought a whole new attitude into the weight room and practice and really rededicated myself. I also saw my body totally change through weight lifting. And then I needed to learn more about nutrition and what kind of fuel my body needed to sustain my workouts. I started to see my body get leaner and stronger.

There are different muscles to focus on when strength training:

Upper: chest, biceps, triceps, and lats (the broad muscles in the back).

Lower: hamstrings, quadriceps, hip abductors and flexors, gluteals, and calves.

Core: abdominals and lower back.

I don't think you need to have a gym membership or a fancy weight set to build muscles: you can do strength training that doesn't involve weights or machines. You can do it through body weight exercises—exercises that use your own body weight to provide resistance. Examples of these exercises are push-ups, sit-ups, lunges, squats, step-ups, and pull-ups. I think these exercises work well for younger athletes and may have less risk of causing injury. You can add weights as you get older.

Sometimes I meet girls who are concerned about getting big muscles and looking bulky. It's not really something to worry about, because most weight training just makes you fit, not super-bulky. I can relate to girls' concerns. When I was in high school, I felt self-conscious because my biceps were so big—bigger than those of a lot of the guys. But I learned to love my muscles because they made me effective on the softball field. Embrace your body and all the amazing things it can do.

*Good fitness habits will
serve you well your whole
life.*

Making Time When You Don't Think You Have Any

I know how hard it can be to find time for a workout. Sometimes when I was a teenager, I would complain about it. I had schoolwork, a social life, or there was a TV show I wanted to watch.

I thought I was busy then. I didn't realize how easy I had it until years later when my son, Ace, came along. When Ace was born, I had to get back in shape in just six weeks for tryouts for the USA national team. It was a crazy schedule, but it set the tone for the early years of Ace's life. Ace was born in May 2006. The Beijing Olympics were scheduled for August 2008. I had to get in shape and stay in shape.

I would get up early in the morning—when it was still dark out—to get in my workouts while Ace and my husband, Casey, were still asleep. I didn't really have a choice; my responsibility was to get in great shape to represent my country and to also be the best mother and wife I could be. I would slip out of bed trying not to wake up anyone else, pull on my workout clothes and running shoes, and head out to the gym. Afterward, I'd meet my catcher and throw. Then I'd come home when my boys were just waking up. My whole life was about being as efficient as I possibly could be.

When I was on the road, sometimes I used Ace as a weight, carrying him while I did lunges up and down the hotel hallways. I did crunches and push-ups in the hotel room while he slept. I used every available moment and every tactic possible to stay fit.

And you know how I managed to do that? Because I had established strong workout habits when I was young. Boy, am I glad I did!

Flexibility

Don't ignore it!

This is an area a lot of young athletes ignore because their bodies bounce back so quickly. But stretching, and keeping your muscles flexible, is an important part of fitness.

I learned the importance of stretching when I was in high school and grew 3½" over a short period of time. My body had trouble adjusting to the new height, and my hamstrings were really tight all the time. I ended up going to physical therapy and learning a lot of useful stretches.

Dynamic stretching is also important. This is stretching involving movement, such as high knees or walking lunges. These are the kind of stretches we do with the national team, and if you come to USA Softball games, you can see us doing our dynamic stretching on the field before we start playing. Stretching is a great way to help prevent injuries, as well.

Yoga is another way to stay flexible and fit. There are a lot of yoga classes available for all ages and levels. Yoga is a great way to learn about body awareness.

RECOVERY AND INJURIES

Recovery is a big part of fitness. Try to schedule days off here and there to let your body rest and avoid getting worn down.

You should also pay close attention to fueling your body as part of the recovery process. An hour or two before a workout, I try to eat something that will be easily digested. Be sure to drink lots of water while you're working out so you don't get dehydrated. In the first 30 minutes after a workout, experts recommend eating food that gives you both some protein and some carbohydrates to replenish your depleted muscles.

It is *very* important to let your body heal if you have an injury. I've seen too many athletes at all levels try to come back too early from an injury for whatever reason: not wanting to miss a big game, feeling pressure to perform from a coach or parent, etc. Often that just leads to a more serious injury.

Listen to your body. If you're hurt, usually the first and best thing you can do is ice your injury. Then be honest with yourself—is this serious? If you have any doubts at all, don't go back in the game. Instead, follow up with a medical specialist. Listen to the expert's advice. Ask all your questions. Follow the treatment plan. Do your rehab exercises.

It's true that sometimes, with medical clearance, you can play through an injury. I did this in college when I had a stress fracture in my throwing forearm. It was painful, but the doctors assured me that I wasn't doing any more damage by playing. Once the season was over, I finally had time to rest it.

If you do have an injury that's going to keep you on the sidelines for a while, stay involved, be supportive of your team, and contribute what you can. I learned that lesson the hard way during the 2004 Olympics. I strained my oblique muscle in the very first game I pitched. Later on at the Games, I was sidelined during the medal round of competition. That was heartbreaking, but I still dug down and tried to be the very best teammate I could be.

If you are injured, don't get discouraged. You'll be back!

And I believe that you might even come back with a greater love for the game. I've seen so many athletes who have suffered an injury return stronger, better, and more hungry for success. I found I learned so much from my injury time because I was observing and learning and discovering how to be a better teammate.

Sometimes an injury truly reignites your fire and your passion.

A Note on ACLs and Concussions

These are two serious forms of injury that are currently getting a lot of attention in terms of their relationships to girls. I think that's a good thing.

Torn ACLs, or Anterior Cruciate Ligaments: The ACL is a key ligament that maintains stability in the knee. This is an injury that girls statistically suffer far more than boys. There are a lot of theories about why this happens—the biomechanics of girls' bodies may put more stress on knees, or their neuromuscular control is different than boys, or hormonal changes could have an impact.

Whatever the reason behind the ACL issue, it's a serious problem. A lot of youth sports leagues have adopted ACL prevention techniques—different exercises that can strengthen the muscles, which can help prevent knee injuries. If you have access to such a program, please take it seriously and do your exercises!

Concussions: Head injuries are another area that we're learning a lot about. There is so much more information on brain injuries today than there ever was before—and the conclusion of medical experts is that there's no such thing as a non-serious hit to the head.

Studies also show that girls sustain more concussions than boys—perhaps 68 percent more often. The reasons for this are unclear, but this is another issue girls need to know about. If you take any kind of hit to the head, pay close attention to how you're feeling. If you have headaches, blurry vision, nausea, or just aren't feeling well, tell someone right away.

PICKING A COACH

This is a big part of the athletic experience for young athletes. Of course, a lot of times you don't get to pick your own coach—you get assigned to a team. But as you get older, and play for more teams, you start to get an idea of what kind of coach works for you.

"My responsibility is leadership, and the minute I get negative, that is going to have an influence on my team."
–Don Shula, football coach

My parents had some bad experiences with the coaches of my older brothers' teams when they played Little League baseball. Usually it was because the coach was also a parent and wanted to make sure their child was the team's star, whether the kid deserved such treatment or not. Sometimes it was that the coach was teaching obviously improper techniques or unsportsmanlike behavior. The result was that one of my brothers didn't even like baseball anymore by the time he got to high school and decided not to play.

That's unfortunate. This is your life. I would urge you not to let a negative experience with one person turn you off something that can be so much fun and so rewarding.

By the time I came along, my parents were pretty sensitive to the problems in youth coaching—all the politics and the potential for poor coaching. So they made sure that they used the lessons they had learned and found the best opportunities for me with coaches who would teach me and help me grow as an athlete.

Sometimes I wasn't happy about their choices. For example, I didn't want to leave a team that was full of my friends. But my parents could see the big picture, and in the end, I realized that their choices were the right ones.

There are also a lot of people out there who want to sell their services to young athletes—everyone from personal trainers to hitting instructors to sports psychologists. Do your homework before hiring someone. Get recommendations from people you trust. Don't assume that just because someone is charging for their services that they're highly qualified.

"The secret of getting ahead is getting started."
—Mark Twain, author

Please understand that picking a good coach doesn't mean finding one who is really nice or who doesn't make demands or who gives you lots of playing time. Those aren't the things that make a good coach.

What makes a good coach? Good coaches try to get the best out of their players. They don't play favorites. They teach proper technique. They don't put winning ahead of doing things the right way.

You might end up having to deal with a difficult coach, which we'll talk about in another chapter. But you can always learn from a challenging situation. I hope you don't let a bad experience with a coach chase you out of sports because there are a lot of really great coaches out there who are dedicated to helping athletes grow and learn.

FIT FOR LIFE

The great thing about establishing fitness habits at a young age is that it will help you for the rest of your life. You're doing yourself a tremendous favor.

Maybe your motivation is to be a better athlete. Maybe your motivation is to feel better and lose weight. Maybe your motivation is to look good in your jeans. Whatever it is, there's never a downside to being physically fit.

I'm so thankful to my dad for always prodding me to do my fitness work and for making sure I got in my workouts. I didn't know it then, but he was helping me establish a routine that would benefit me for the rest of my life.

Jennie's Tips for a Great Workout

1. Don't procrastinate. Just lace up those shoes and get moving!

2. Find a partner. If you are accountable to someone else, you won't have excuses. And you'll have more fun!

3. Hydrate. Remember to drink plenty of water while you're working out.
4. Listen to music! Get an armband for your iPod and load it with your favorite up-tempo songs. Or just put on music and dance around your house. Dancing around our apartment at Arizona always got our blood moving.
5. Be organized. Schedule your workout ahead of time when you're planning your day. Fill out a journal so you can keep track of what you're doing.

Chapter 4

Accepting Who You Are:
Body Image, Dieting, and Nutrition

When I was nine years old, I told my dad I was quitting softball.

I loved the sport. I had so much fun playing it. So my father was naturally puzzled about why I suddenly wanted to quit.

"Look," I said, pointing to my shoulders.

My right arm—my pitching arm—was huge. Overdeveloped. Muscled. My left arm was regular-sized. I thought I looked like a freak. I was getting to an age where I was becoming self-conscious about the way I looked. I didn't want to play softball if it made me look weird.

My dad, who restored cars and could build pretty much anything, went to work in the garage. He ended up inventing the Finch Windmill, a groundbreaking piece of exercise equipment that allowed me to work out both sides of my body and helped even things out. It's something I still use to this day and a device that many others use for training. So that was a positive side effect of my temporary negative body image.

But like lots of girls, I always had issues with how I looked. I've done some modeling and was even named to an ESPN list of "Hottest Athletes," and *People* magazine's "50 Most Beautiful People," so sometimes people assume that I've always been confident and self-assured about myself.

That is a very wrong assumption.

My dad invented the Finch Windmill for me—I still use it!

> *"Always be a first-rate version of yourself, instead of a second-rate version of somebody else."*
> —Judy Garland, actress

FEELING AWKWARD

Growing up I hated how tall I was. I towered over boys and was certain that I'd never find anyone tall enough to marry. I was chunky, and I never wanted to show off my body. I wore a size 13 in junior high, and all the sizes in the stores stopped at 11. I hated going shopping.

When I could find clothes, they didn't fit right. They didn't look cute or stylish on me, the way the fashions looked in magazines. I had big muscles, which were great for softball but not—in my opinion at the time—very pretty. My feet were like gigantic boats on the end of my legs. I wore a size 11 shoe and was always trying to squish my feet into size 10s. I wanted to be petite. I wanted to be prettier. I wanted to look like other girls.

Negative body image is something us girls really have to work hard to overcome. I talk to so many beautiful young girls who feel like they're too fat. Or too tall. Or too *something*. They hate their skin. Or their hair. Or their nose. They feel awkward and ugly.

And even though they look beautiful to me, I understand where they're coming from and why they feel that way.

EXTERIOR BEAUTY VS. INTERIOR HAPPINESS

Girls are bombarded with images of what is "beautiful." They hear boys talk about who's "hot." We all see images of models and celebrities and think that's what we're all supposed to look like. But those images are enhanced by lighting, makeup artists, cosmetics, fake tans, hair dye, and sometimes by plastic surgery. They're not a realistic goal for anyone to shoot for. Believe me—sometimes I see photos of myself and I can't believe them. Those photographers can work magic!

"The thing I like about my body is that it's strong. I can move furniture. I can ride my horse. I can play basketball.... It's a well-functioning machine."
—Cindy Crawford, model

Through my softball career, I had a chance to meet a lot of celebrities and be exposed to the world of Hollywood. And I've seen a lot of unhappiness emanating from some of the most beautiful people in the world, people who have everything you could ever dream of in terms of fame and material wealth. The lesson I've learned from my excursions into that world is that the old adage is true: Money—and I'll add beauty and fame to the saying—doesn't buy happiness. True happiness comes from within.

I wish I could tell every girl who has self-doubts about her looks not to worry! Work on what's on the inside—the things that make you passionate and happy and fulfilled. When you're feeling great on the inside, the world will notice.

One thing I have learned is that the most beautiful people are the ones who are confident. People who feel good about themselves and accept themselves are attractive. That shines through to others.

Softball was a way for me to feel confident about myself. It was a way for me to learn to love my muscles—they helped me be a strong player. And my height—it helped me pitch better. Softball not only helped me accept my body, but it also helped me learn to take better care of my body.

In truth, your concerns about your looks and body never go away. I know mine haven't. It's something I work on everyday. But I find that focusing on ways to make myself a better person makes how I look feel less important. The less we focus on ourselves, the easier it becomes to accept yourself.

DIET, WEIGHT, AND NUTRITION

We didn't eat very well when I was growing up. I had two working parents and two older brothers who could each consume about a million-and-a-half calories a day. We had a freezer full of junk food, bagel dogs, and French fries. The goal was quick, easy, and filling. I was on the bigger side when I was a kid—chunky and thick—so all that junk food wasn't helping.

When I was a teenager and my brothers had moved out, I started worrying more about my diet. For a while, I was obsessed about having a fat-free diet. That didn't mean I had a healthy diet. I would gorge on pretzels because they were "fat free." I would eat Skittles to get some energy because they were "fat free." I would read boxes and wrappers to

I felt like I was too tall and too chunky when I was young.

> *"You don't have to cook fancy or complicated masterpieces—just good food from fresh ingredients."*
> —Julia Child, chef

make sure the products were "fat free." Meanwhile I was overloading on carbohydrates and sugar—not exactly a healthy way to go.

When I first went to college, I simply ate everything in sight! I was living on my own and lazy about shopping or cooking. My roommate, Toni, and I were the worst shoppers; when our parents would come to visit, they wondered if we had any real food or just snacks.

I was also working out hard and lifting weights for the first time—which meant I was starving all the time. Instead of being smart about my choices, I ate whatever was easy and filling. And I gained 20 pounds my freshman year!

That was a big lesson. I had to work really hard that summer to get the extra weight off and get in the shape I needed to be in to play college ball at the highest level. I learned to save the high-calorie stuff for treats and not for everyday eating.

Life would have been a lot easier if I had just used some common sense about eating a healthy, balanced diet. Toni and I learned to make sure we had nutritious food available so that if we were starving we could grab something healthy rather than a fast-food burger.

But in some ways I'm happy I wasn't too obsessed about food. I've seen how concerns over weight and dieting can spiral out of control.

One of my teammates in college became anorexic. She had been an outgoing, beautiful girl—who, by the way, wasn't overweight at all—and she got sicker and sicker, falling into a deeper and darker hole. She tried to keep it a secret, but it's hard to keep secrets on a team full of girls. We all could see what was going on. Sometimes she couldn't even practice because she was so weak from starving herself. Her whole life became about eating—or not eating—and hiding her disease. It was one of the saddest and most frightening things I've ever seen.

Anorexia is an illness a lot of girls deal with—and it can be a deadly one. The most important thing is to *get help* if you feel like you're spinning out of control, or if you feel like a friend is in danger. Talk to a parent or a counselor or a coach or your doctor. It's not something to be taken lightly—the human body is an engine that runs on fuel. Without fuel it can shut down completely.

Don't put your health at risk for some crazy ideal assuming *skinniness = happiness*. It really doesn't.

I'm the Chairman of an organization called 'nPlay, which is a foundation organized to fight the epidemic of childhood obesity. Our mission is to support physical education and activity programs in low-income areas that have the highest rates of childhood obesity. This is another big problem that can lead to lifelong health problems.

I find it frustrating that at the same time there is growing awareness about the importance of fitness and nutrition, school and community physical education programs are at risk because of budget cuts.

But the reality is that with these cuts we all have to find our own way to get moving and make healthy food choices. I'm here to cheer you on. I know you can do it.

WE'RE ALL DIFFERENT

Softball gave me a path for dealing with all sorts of body issues. It helped me stay active. It helped me learn how to properly fuel my body and to make the right nutrition choices. And it helped me feel good about my body and the way I look.

What I love most about my sport is that players come in all shapes and sizes: tiny, tall, chunky, thin, well-muscled, and not so

> *"Happiness cannot come from without.*
> *It must come from within."*
> —Helen Keller, author and activist

Jennie's Recipes: Favorite Healthy Snacks

Peanut butter and everything: Peanut butter is a great source of protein and one that has saved me countless times in foreign countries. When I couldn't find anything that was familiar or nutritious to eat, I could count on a peanut butter and jelly sandwich to keep me going. I always pack a jar of peanut butter on long trips. At home, I like to put peanut butter on an apple or on a bagel.

Greek yogurt, fruit, and granola: Greek yogurt is thick, creamy, and another great source of protein. Mixed with a little low-fat granola and some fresh fruit, it is a filling and delicious breakfast or snack that can get you through a long workout.

Hard-boiled eggs: Can you see a theme here? My quick snacks pack a protein punch. Hard-boiled eggs are so easy to make and easy to transport. Of course, you don't want to eat too many of them because eggs have a lot of cholesterol. But they're a great way to get some protein. I even like to make a hard-boiled egg sandwich—slicing an egg onto bread with some salt and pepper and a tiny bit of light mayonnaise. I add spinach to get even more vitamins and minerals.

Pasta salad: Cook triple-colored Rigatoni noodles. Drain and mix with cut up broccoli, carrots, red onion, and black olives. Toss with Italian salad dressing and some rice vinegar. My mom used to make a big batch of this before a tournament, and we would put it in the cooler and eat it all weekend. The pasta is filling, and the vegetables make it healthy. For a variety, mix in tuna or chicken. You can use quinoa pasta. Quinoa is a grain that has protein.

Fruit of any kind: Apples, pears, apricots, peaches, bananas, berries, cut-up melon, and papaya. Easy to transport and delicious!

I love sweating in my uniform but I also love getting dressed up for a big night out. (AP Images)

much. And it's not just my sport. I loved the Opening Ceremonies of the Olympics because I walked side by side with tiny gymnasts, tall basketball players, and powerful shot-putters. We were all Team USA teammates, all representing the best of our sports, and we were all totally different with different gifts and talents.

There's not one way to look to be beautiful or successful. We're not cookie cutters of each other—nor are we supposed to be. How boring would the world be if everyone looked the same? We all have our individual beauty—I believe that's the way God made us—and we should celebrate that.

I have to laugh to think that I might have quit my sport because I was concerned about the way it made me look. If I had done that, think of all the wonderful things I would have missed!

Jennie's Tips for Diet and Nutrition

1. Get involved with your family's food decisions. Help with making the shopping list and the meal planning, help with the shopping and cooking. Sometimes Mom and Dad are just too busy or overwhelmed and are looking for the quickest way to get food on the table. You can't just rely on your parents. Take some accountability for your own body.

2. Read labels! Fresh, natural products are best. Try to stay away from processed food, products with lots of ingredients you don't recognize, or products that are full of something you know for sure is unhealthy for you. There are so many more healthy choices these days than there used to be.

3. Plan ahead. The times I find I make poor diet decisions are when I'm starving and can't wait to eat. But that doesn't have to happen. I can predict that I'm going to be hungry after a hard workout, so I always try to make sure I have something nutritious to eat: a yogurt, a bagel, a banana. Getting something in my stomach prevents me from making impulsive choices—like deciding that extra-large fries are exactly what I need!

4. Don't obsess about numbers on a scale. Your weight fluctuates day to day. Muscles weigh more than fat, so when you start getting in shape, your weight might not drop dramatically. Shoot for a healthy range, not a target number.

5. Reward yourself. No one wants to deprive themselves all the time. That just leads to negative feelings and unrealistic goals. But make sure that you have balance. Food that is tasty but may not be not the healthiest should be a treat, not an everyday menu item. That makes it taste even better!

6. Make sure your diet is full of color!

II. MIND

Chapter 5

Busting Stereotypes:
Why Are People Always Trying to Label Us?

Sometimes I feel like I need to check the mirror to make sure I don't have a sign posted on my forehead, such as

Hottest Athlete

PRETTY GIRL   Tomboy

WORKING MOM

All my life, I've had labels hung on me. People judge the exterior and assume they know what's on the inside. And it's not just me: I see the same thing happening to my teammates and other female athletes all the time. It's probably happened to you.

For some reason, people want to stick us all in easy-to-label boxes: jock, brain, slacker, pretty girl.

53

"Be who you are and say what you feel because those who mind don't matter and those who matter don't mind."
–Dr. Seuss, author

BUSTING STEREOTYPES

I've always tried to bust out of those stereotypes. I'm considered a really feminine player in a sport that is sometimes considered macho. I was named one of ESPN's "Hottest Athletes," but that superficial label came when I was dominating opposing hitters with nasty pitches. I don't like it when other people tell me who or what I'm supposed to be.

There's not any one way to be. I feel very fortunate that I have lived through a time when stereotypes about female athletes were being challenged and changed. It's okay for great athletes to be super-girly. Or not. Beautiful women can have big muscles. As females, we shouldn't let ourselves be stereotyped or boxed in.

Labels are a way to pressure people to conform. Criticism is another way. That kind of pressure is harshest in middle school and high school. If that's your age group, please be assured it won't always be like this!

As you get older and more confident about who you are, you pay less attention to those kinds of labels and to the peer pressure to fit into someone else's notion of who you should be.

But people still want to stick labels on others, even outside of high school. I've heard lots of assumptions about my sport and about myself. While some labels are meant as a compliment—like "Hottest Athlete"—I wanted to make sure people knew about the "Athlete" part first! That's what I've worked hard for.

THE "PRETTY GIRL" SYNDROME

When I started playing sports, I always put ribbons in my braids or ponytails. My father was the one who did my hair for me before games when I was little because my mom was often at work. He always said that just because a girl plays sports doesn't mean she can't be feminine. So that became my motto, too.

In truth, I wasn't super-girly. I was the younger sister of two rowdy brothers, and I wanted to be just like them. I was such a tomboy, the kind of girl who would rather be rolling around in the dirt than inside playing with dolls. So I kind of liked the fact that I became known as the "pitcher with the ribbons in her hair." It was a way to balance my two sides.

I never felt like I was pretty when I was growing up—I was always too big and bulky, towering over all the boys. I started feeling better about my size when I grew really fast in high school—it helped me lose some of my baby fat. But I still wasn't crazy about being so tall.

Like any teenage girl, I was always concerned about how I looked, especially when I was playing softball. I liked making sure my hair was just right. I liked wearing makeup in games. I liked the contrast between being a tough-as-nails athlete and a hot-pink-on-my-nails girl. I liked that balance. It was right for me.

My teammate, Toni, and I used to always spray perfume on our game jerseys—just a goofy, super-girly thing we liked to do. We did it on our travel team in high school, and we did it when we were teammates at Arizona. It became our little ritual—one I kept going right up until my retirement game.

When I was young, there wasn't a lot of softball equipment available to girls. We had to buy boys' equipment. So when I started working

"Someone's opinion of you does not have to become your reality."
—Les Brown, motivational speaker

I want to be known for being a dominating athlete. (AP Images)

with the athletic equipment company Mizuno, it was so exciting for me to be involved in making girl-centric changes to products. One of the executives asked his wife if she thought he would be crazy to have a pink softball glove. She told him that she thought it was crazy that no one had made one until then! I agreed and was so excited about the idea.

So Mizuno made a line of Jennie Finch gear with pink accents: batting gloves, bats, sliding shorts. I love it! We call it "fierce pink," and Mizuno is committed to making sure that we're not sacrificing performance for style. Mizuno's motto is "Serious Performance." I love that 10- or 12-year-old girls can walk into a sporting goods store and see softball equipment that they know is designed especially for them to fit their proportions and the needs of their sport. I never had that chance when I was a kid.

My girly exterior housed a fiercely competitive athlete. But I found that people looked at my ribbons and my makeup and my blond hair and made a lot of assumptions about who I was. They thought that I was just a "pretty girl," that I didn't work too hard on the field, that I didn't like to sweat, that I was a prima donna.

That was really upsetting to me. I heard the things that other players and even some of my teammates said about me behind my back.

When I was a freshman in high school, a girl one year ahead of me told the seniors that I was a snob. That happened again when I was at Arizona—a teammate said some nasty things about me, and I only found out because my friends told me. She was basing her opinion of me on what she thought I would be like rather than who I really was. It was very unfair.

It hurts when people talk about you. It really forced me to practice mental toughness.

And it motivated me to work even harder. I was busting my butt, sweating, hurting, and giving 100 percent just like everyone else. Eventually, the truth comes out, and my other teammates quickly saw that I was nothing like what those girls said I was.

My teammates also found out that despite the makeup and ribbons, I wasn't exactly a delicate little flower. I grew up with two older brothers, so there isn't much that can gross me out. As any of my friends can tell you, I am not really all that girly! My roommates Mackenzie and Toni used to say, "Hey Jennie, how about taking a shower!"

I suppose I could have stopped wearing makeup or ribbons or anything pink to try to prove to those critics that I was just as tough and fierce as any other player. But why should I have done that?

Why couldn't I just be myself?

MEAN GIRLS AND JUDGMENTAL BOYS

Girls are under a lot of pressure from both sides: from other girls and the boys who pass judgment on girls. The best thing you can do is ignore all the labels other people want to hang on you.

I know that's easier said than done.

Sometimes meanness stems from jealousy and insecurity. If a person can belittle someone else he or she can make him- or herself feel better. There have been all sorts of studies written about this—but that doesn't make dealing with it any easier.

It definitely hurt my feelings when other girls assumed that because I looked a certain way I wasn't a tough athlete. Or if they wanted me not to do well because they felt I was getting too much attention. I tried to ignore that stuff and just be the best teammate I could be. But, of course, it stung inside.

The best defense is to pick your friends wisely. Find friends you can trust and try not to be concerned about being with the most "popular" group.

I feel fortunate that I've always had lots of different kinds of friends. In high school, there were five of us that were best friends. We called ourselves the Bomb Squad—because we were the bomb! I know, that's pretty ridiculous, but we loved being goofy together. We were all from different ethnic backgrounds; when we were together it was like a rainbow. We all had different interests. We've all gone on to different careers. But we were and still are incredibly tight friends. It was a wonderful lesson for me; not everybody has to be the same to form close bonds.

The other members of the Bomb Squad didn't play softball, which was great. They were a safe haven away from the pressures of softball, and they didn't have any competitive feelings toward me. I knew they were my friends no matter whether I had a good game or a bad game.

"The biggest men and women with the biggest ideas can be shot down by the smallest men and women with the smallest minds. Think big anyway."
—Kent M. Keith, motivational speaker

The Bomb Squad dressed up for "Nerd Day" in high school.

A lot of the pressure girls feel is because of boys. Girls can be mean because they feel competitive over boys. Boys have a power over girls that I don't even think they realize. They decide which girls are "hot" and which ones aren't. I've seen girls change their lives or suppress their lively, funny personalities because they think it will make them more attractive to boys. Don't ever let a boy or anyone else define who you are!

The one boy I went out with in high school knew that softball was my top priority. I wouldn't go out on a Friday night if I had an early morning game. If he didn't like that, too bad. That was who I was. And true friends will respect you!

My husband, Casey, is a professional athlete. We met because of softball. He was on the Arizona Diamondbacks, who hold their spring training in Tucson. He and another player—Luis Gonzalez—came out to one of our games. Casey saw me pitch and decided he wanted to meet me. It turned out that we went to the same hair stylist to get our hair cut. He found out when I had my next appointment and sent four dozen roses to the salon!

I was overwhelmed. I had been dating someone else at the time, so I turned down Casey's dinner invitation. But I felt really conflicted. My other relationship wasn't going anywhere, and my friend, Toni, had been asking me why I didn't end it. I knew it was time, so I officially ended my other relationship and agreed to go out with Casey—our first date was a group date.

We clicked right away. Even though he's a country boy from a ranch in Southern Louisiana and I'm from a cul-de-sac in Southern California, we found we had so much in common—not only our sports backgrounds but also our values and our likes. We even both grew up playing a card game called Canasta! It seemed like a sign.

We started going out right around the time my softball career began getting a lot of notice. I had just come off an NCAA championship season and was in the middle of what would be a 60-game win streak.

I was doing all sorts of interviews and appearances, was invited to the ESPYs, and was hired to do a weekly segment on *This Week in Baseball*. The hype for the 2004 Olympics was starting, and I was becoming one of the faces of the national team. All that attention is the kind of thing that could make some guys very jealous and possessive. And me too! I never liked the singled-out attention—I played a team sport.

But Casey is totally confident in himself. If it bothers him when people constantly bring up his "famous wife," he doesn't show it. When he was a rookie, his teammates made him dress up as me (on major league teams there is usually one travel day early in the season reserved for some silly rookie hazing). He went along with the prank, putting on

Here I am with Casey and Ace, my super supportive guys.

a Jennie Finch No. 27 USA Softball jersey and a blond wig. He's a very good sport.

Casey admits that he had some stereotypes when it came to girls playing sports; he didn't think that any girl could be as driven about her sport as I am. He says I'm even more intense than he is. He also got to the point where he wouldn't catch my drop ball anymore because it banged up his shins so badly. He'll proudly show people the big discolored spot on his shin left by my pitches.

Jennie's Top Female Athletes

Billie Jean King—I feel so privileged to have gotten to know one of the great pioneers for women athletes. Billie Jean has done—and continues to do—so much for women in all of sports, founding the Women's Sports Foundation and fighting for equality for girls and women who play sports. She is amazing!

Lisa Fernandez—Lisa was my idol growing up. I waited for hours to get her autograph and watched her workout every chance I could. And then I was privileged to play with her. She is the fiercest, toughest competitor I've ever met! She and I had our sons around the same time, and we spent a lot of time together figuring out how to be moms and play our sport. I feel so blessed to call her a good friend today.

Mia Hamm—Mia changed her sport. She helped put women's soccer on the map and went beyond her own sport to become an example of a driven competitor. She was always such a great role model, a great teammate, and such a graceful player with the heart of a lion! Mia made it cool to be a female athlete.

Lisa Leslie—Lisa not only did so much for basketball, she also proved that you don't have to stick women athletes in one box. She's a model and an actress and took her sport mainstream. She left quite a legacy.

Annika Sorenstam—I love Annika because she let her golf do the talking. She was the face of women's golf and was such a picture of consistent excellence. She's soft-spoken and didn't really enjoy all the attention she received, but she always handled it with grace.

Serena Williams—Serena made it okay for a beautiful woman to be powerful and strong. She's an intense competitor. And she and her sister, Venus, also prove that they have so many different talents in addition to tennis.

I am incredibly blessed to have found a guy like Casey. To have a husband who supports my sports and lets me be myself, and who encourages me to challenge myself and travel the world—with our baby boy—in pursuit of my dreams. He hasn't tried to make me conform to any preconceived notions about who he thought his wife should be.

SHEDDING LABELS

One of the things I love best about my sport is that you don't have to be any particular type to play this game. In softball, athletes come in all shapes and sizes—and from all different backgrounds and attitudes. You can wear pink ribbons in your hair, or you can buzz off all your hair. You can be whoever you want to be.

One of my best friends in the whole world is Crystl Bustos, who was my teammate on the USA national team for so many years. She was usually my roommate on the road. She is a strong, powerful woman, an intimidating slugger, covered in tattoos—from the outside she and I look like opposites. Yet we are such good friends. She has an absolute heart of gold. She would play with Ace on the road and color beautiful Winnie the Pooh posters for him. She's a softy.

If you were to put the two of us next to each other, you'd never assume that we'd be so close. I'm sure we would be tagged with really different labels, based on what we look like from the outside.

And you know what? Those labels would be dead wrong.

They usually are.

"Labels are for filing. Labels are for clothing. Labels are not for people."
—Martina Navratilova, tennis champion

Jennie's Tips for Busting Stereotypes

1. Don't use them yourself. Get to know people before you make assumptions about what they're really like.

2. Stand up for what you believe in. If you hear people talking behind someone's back and saying something you don't think is true, don't just sit bt quietly. Your silence will be taken as a sign that you agree. Don't just go along with the crowd because it's the easiest thing to do.

3. Be true to yourself. If you want to wear ribbons in your hair, do it. If you want to cut your hair really short, go for it. If you want to spend your weekend reading Russian novels or listening to classical music, that's your choice. You don't have to be like everyone else. That's what makes the world an interesting place.

4. Pick your friends wisely. The best buffer against the power of mean people is having friends you can trust and who allow you to be yourself. If you find yourself hanging around people who are mean or critical or who are doing things you know you shouldn't do, it's time to make a change. It's better to hang out by yourself than with people who are a bad influence.

5. Remember that middle school and high school won't last forever. Be concerned about figuring out who *you* are and what's going to be the best course for *you* rather than trying to fit in with people you might not even know in a few years.

Chapter 6

The High Wire Act:
How to Keep Your Balance

When I was about 13, I used to lie in my bed and pray for a "normal life."

I'm not kidding.

I used to pray, "Lord, please just make me be normal. I want to be like other kids and go to the beach and slumber parties and the mall."

Obviously, I wasn't doing a great job of balancing my life back then. My personal scales felt like they were tipped too heavily toward softball. And even though I loved my sport, I felt like I was missing out on so much else.

In fact, the friends I had growing up would probably laugh out loud at the thought of me giving advice about finding balance in life because I had a hard time doing it myself. But looking back, I think I actually had more balance than I thought.

A SOFTBALL PASSION

I was a softball player. We were a softball family. It consumed us all year round. Our fashions changed with whatever team I was on at the time. Our life was molded around the softball schedule.

My parents and I would get up early on a Saturday morning—and I mean *really* early, like 5:30 AM—and load up the cooler full of drinks and food, pack up the orange 1979 Ford, and head off to a softball tournament. Sometimes our car would be decorated with streamers and messages painted on the window—words that only my teammates would understand. We wouldn't get back until late Sunday night.

After a while, my school friends stopped calling me to ask me to sleep over or hang out at the mall. They knew I probably couldn't because I was off playing softball. And after so many answers of, "No, I can't do that," the calls and invitations just stopped coming. Even my older brothers would joke that the world stopped when it was time for softball. Which seemed like all the time: 24/7, 52 weeks a year, year after year.

Sometimes it seemed too much, especially when I learned from my friends at school on Monday about some fun I missed over the weekend when I had been on the softball field. But looking back on it, I'm actually thrilled I didn't have the "normal life" that I was praying for.

Instead of hanging out or sleeping in, I was doing something that felt truly special. I had great friendships with a bunch of girls who were goal-driven like I was.

We cultivated our friendships on the softball field, instead of at the mall. I did have different kinds of slumber parties—my teammates and I would hang out with each other in the lobbies and hallways of hotels during tournaments. We'd celebrate birthdays together with parties at

"Each one of us has a fire in our heart for something. It's our goal in life to find it and keep it lit."
—Mary Lou Retton, Olympic gold medalist

Softball gave me so many unique and special experiences. (AP Images)

restaurants or picnics at a nearby park. And yes, we'd even manage to sometimes go to the mall or movies between softball games.

We didn't go on many family vacations, but we actually saw a lot of the country because of travel for softball tournaments. And we had great, quality family time together—something I realize now is a rare and special thing.

The truth was, I was doing all the so-called "normal" things—just not in the same way as some other girls. The biggest difference was I was also having an incredible softball experience. It wasn't "normal"—but abnormal in a very good way. For me, softball was unique and special.

It was hard to see all those benefits when I was 13. All I saw back then was what I was missing.

LEARNING TO JUGGLE

What I didn't know when I was younger was that I was learning a lesson that will stay with me for the rest of my life: how to juggle priorities. Some of the balls I was juggling—the mall, slumber parties, sleeping in—couldn't stay in the air...not if I was going to prevent my most precious ones—like softball, school, and church—from dropping.

So I did the best I could. I did my homework in the car on the way to practice. I snoozed in the back seat on the way to tournaments. I went to church in my softball uniform—I don't think God minded.

And as it turns out, I was able to do a lot of things besides softball. When I was in high school, I had a really close group of non-softball friends who were also really busy—with cheerleading and soccer and

"If we did all the things that we are capable of doing, we would literally astound ourselves."
—Thomas Edison, inventor

other activities. The five of us in the Bomb Squad all ran for student government offices. My best friends were all really good students, so it pushed me to work harder at academics. I played volleyball and basketball for my high school teams in addition to softball. I also had a boyfriend when I was a senior.

So it wasn't as though I had sacrificed my entire life. My childhood wasn't actually ruined because I missed Saturday afternoons at the mall and Trisha Smith's birthday party at the skating rink.

But trust me, I know it is really hard and stressful to juggle all that you're expected to do. With Facebook, cell phones, laptops, and whatever comes next, it's only getting harder to keep up with everything. There's so much information, and it's all so instantaneous.

Your friends expect you to be available all the time, your parents expect you to be on top of everything, your coaches and teachers expect high levels of performance. There's a lot of competition in every part of your life.

You probably feel pressure to:
✓ Get good grades
✓ Do extracurricular activities
✓ Be good at sports
✓ Look pretty
✓ Be stylish
✓ Be up to date on everything in pop culture
✓ Be a good daughter
✓ Be a good friend
✓ Be attractive to boys
✓ Practice your religion
✓ Earn some money
✓ Prepare for your future

That's a lot! It's exhausting even thinking about it, let alone actually *doing* it.

The simplest advice I can give you for managing all the juggling is to stay organized. Use a calendar or your homework planner to keep

Once Ace came along I really had to learn how to juggle all the demands in my life.

track of deadlines and commitments. Make lists—both a daily and weekly to-do list. Stick up Post-its as reminders. Make sure your parents know what your schedule is to help with their own planning. And don't sweat the small stuff. Don't be too hard on yourself if something falls through the cracks.

Life is one long balancing act. Learning how to multitask and juggle is a skill that will serve you forever. I *really* learned that when my son, Ace, was born.

Everything that came before seemed easy compared to the year I became a mother. Here was my to-do list: learn to be a great mom, play Olympic-level softball, be a loving and supportive wife, stay in great shape, be a good friend and daughter, and represent my sport proudly. I still have a crazy schedule even though I retired from playing. I give speeches and clinics and run camps all around the country. I'm always getting on a plane—sometimes I feel like my sanity is dependent on the airline's flight schedule.

My husband, Casey, just looks at me and shakes his head sometimes at the unpredictability of my schedule. I really do feel like I'm on a high wire trying to get from one priority to the next. I'm grateful I learned how to deal with multiple demands when I was younger.

And even though life gets crazy and busy, don't forget to enjoy the moment!

"Seek out that particular mental attribute which makes you feel most deeply alive, along with which comes the inner voice which says, 'This is the real me,' and follow it."
—James Truslow Adams, American writer

Dealing With Stress

In recent years, there have been many studies on teenage and adolescent stress. Studies find that more girls than boys report experiencing frequent stress and that young people from urban areas and middle-income households are the most susceptible.

The American Academy of Pediatrics has established some suggestions for how to manage stress.

- Tackle the problem, rather than ignore it. Fixing a problem can make you feel better. And getting to work on a problem rather than procrastinating can actually make you worry less.
- Tackle your problem by breaking it down into small manageable tasks.
- Make a to-do list and cross out each item as you complete it.
- Avoid things and people that bring you down, upset you, or that you know are potential trouble.
- Let some things go. Don't waste your energy worrying about what you can't change.

PRIORITIZING

How can you survive the high-wire act? Prioritize. Obviously, softball was a big priority for me, and I had to make everything else fit around it. Sometimes it was stressful, but mostly it was fun. I loved playing.

When something stops being enjoyable, you might think about dropping it down your priority list. Well, except for school of course—that can't become a low priority! But if an extracurricular activity is more stressful than fun, it probably should be reevaluated.

Maybe you've always danced and played the flute and played tennis. But if you find you can't keep doing all three, you have to be practical

- Take care of your body.
- Exercise regularly to manage your stress.
- Eat well.
- Sleep well.
- Learn to relax. Breathe deeply. Find comfortable ways of sitting.
- Manage your emotions.
- Take instant vacations by visualizing favorite places.
- Make time for yourself.
- Take time doing your favorite hobby or something you love, like being with your dog.
- Release your emotions. Find an outlet in the arts (singing, dancing, music), write in a journal, pray, have a good laugh or cry, or talk things out with friends. Don't keep everything inside.
- Make the world a better place. You can find stress relief by looking outside of yourself by volunteering, working for the environment, or helping a family member.

For more information, go to www.aap.org/stress.

and decide which one to give up. A starting point is figuring out which is the least enjoyable to you.

When you were little, you probably tried a bunch of different activities, encouraged by your parents who wanted you to learn about lots of different things and pick up different skills. But it's not realistic to think that you can keep doing every single activity you ever started. If you tried to do that, you'd be too busy to eat or sleep, and you'd never really get good at anything. And while it's nice to have a lot of skills, it's also terrific to really feel that you're excelling at something.

As you get older, you will have a better idea of what you like and where your passion and interests lie. As school becomes more demanding and you start thinking about your future, it might be time to whittle down your commitments and focus on just a few things.

You need to listen to your heart when you're making tough decisions. If you don't love playing the piano, but your parents really, really want you to keep playing, you probably need to have an honest talk with them. If I didn't feel passionate about softball and was only doing it to keep my dad happy, I would have been miserable. Luckily, I loved it, too.

Ask people around you for advice when making tough decisions, people like your parents and siblings who love you and have your best interests in mind.

Remember that dropping an activity doesn't mean that you're giving it up forever. If you've always danced but find you don't have time for practice and lessons, your ability will still be there. You can always pick up dance again when you have more time for it. Or after a break, you may learn that you miss it so much that you're even more eager to get back to it. Then it needs to move up the priority list.

For me, softball was my priority and my focus. I found a way—with the full support of my family—to play at a very high level. If your sport is your passion, find a way to make it work. If it's not your passion, perhaps you could play at a different level (for example, recreation league instead of club level), or take a break from it for a while.

If you choose to take a break, I encourage you to make sure you still find time for physical activity. View sports or your workout time

"Of course I want to be No. 1. But being happy and healthy is the most important thing."
—Venus Williams, tennis champion

Take the opportunity to get outside, away from a screen, and play!

as a little vacation from all the other things you have going on in life—from studying and social pressures and parents' constant advice.

Physical activity can be a welcome brain break. It's a chance to get your heart rate up, get a sweat going, be with friends, and run around like a little kid. Sure, playing sports can cause stress because of the time commitment, but it can also relieve stress. And it can provide a nice balance in your crazy life, one that gets you away from the laptop or the algebra book or the fashion wars at school and give you a chance to breathe.

> *"The only normal people are the ones you don't know very well."*
> —Alfred Adler, physician

After a long day in school, I used to look forward to getting out on the practice field. Getting dirty. Getting sweaty. I didn't have to worry about what I was wearing, or what boys were saying, or which girl might have been mean that day at lunch. It was a relief. And when I got home and it was time to study, I felt refreshed and ready to focus.

BURN OUT

Teenagers are under a lot of stress these days. There have been a lot of studies done on the competitive pressure young people feel.

If you're feeling stressed out, unhappy, and unable to sleep, you need to get some help from an expert. Such feelings can lead to destructive behaviors like cutting, anorexia, and drug and alcohol abuse. And those behaviors can only lead to bigger problems and more stress. It can become a vicious cycle. The adults in your life are there to help you. Please don't feel alone.

If it feels like things are getting to be too much for you to handle, take an honest inventory of your life. Think about what is important to you. Have truthful conversations with your parents, coaches, and teachers. Find a way to connect more deeply with your real interests and passions. This is your life: you can't live someone else's life.

Sometimes you have to be able to say no. It's always easier to say yes when there's an invitation or a schedule change or a request for your time. But for every "yes," you need to find a "no" so that you don't become overcommitted. Try to be realistic about your academic workload; you may not have to take all Advanced Placement and

Honors classes. Scale back to a manageable load. Ask your parents for help in organizing your schedule.

Also make sure you have some down time. Time with your family. Time for sleep—your body needs the rest. And time to simply let your mind wander and relax.

WHAT'S NORMAL?

What I didn't know when I was 13 and praying for a "normal life" is that there really isn't such a thing. Everyone is different. Every family is different.

Most importantly, each of us has our own passion and our own individual talents.

In order to be the best I could be, I had to sacrifice some things. But it takes hard work to realize your dreams. And the truth is, I'd do it all over again in a heartbeat.

I encourage you to find your passion. Listen to your heart. And whatever your dreams are, pursue them. Who knows where they might take you?

Jennie's Tips for Learning How to Juggle

1. Follow your heart! When you make a priority list of all the things you need to do, think about what makes *you* the happiest. Don't just fill your schedule with things you *should* do or *have* to do.

2. Stay organized. Make lists, use your planner and the family calendar, stick reminder Post-its around your room.

3. Don't get caught up in what everyone else is doing. You don't have to take all honors classes just because your friends are. You don't have to go out for drama because that's what everyone else is doing. Know yourself. Know what you can handle. There's a difference between challenging yourself and pushing yourself too far.

4. Focus on others. When you look outside yourself, some of your stress will vanish.

5. Unplug. This is harder and harder to do, but studies show that sitting in front of a screen can be fatiguing and stressful. Find time to be away from your computer, game system, TV, or phone.

6. Take care of your body. Get enough sleep—eight hours a night if possible. And schedule time for exercise. Use your workout as a much-needed brain break. Think of it as a time when you can escape all the other pressures of life, relieve stress, and have fun.

Chapter 7

What's the Payoff?
Where Will Sports Get Me?

The first letter arrived when I was 14.

I came home from school and it was sitting there on the kitchen table. The white envelope. The blue and yellow print on the return address. The name: UCLA.

Until that moment, I didn't know that a rectangular paper envelope could fill a person with such giddiness and butterflies.

My hands were shaking while I opened it. It said something basic like, "We admire your athletic achievements and are interested in staying in touch." But to me, those typed words felt like a life-changing promise.

I hadn't really thought about college softball until the day that envelope came in the mail. I had focused on high school and travel ball. The future seemed really far away. But college was the next step. And it started with that envelope. Then other envelopes started arriving, until pretty soon we had so many that we had to get a box to store them all.

It hadn't been my original goal when I started playing softball as a little girl. There are some parents who push their kids into sports, dreaming of a full-ride scholarship or some sort of grand financial benefit. Not my parents. Not me. I had just wanted to play softball, to have fun, and to be the best player I could be.

DREAMS AND GOALS

When I was young, my original dream was to play for the Los Angeles Dodgers. I loved going to Dodgers games. I wore Dodgers second baseman Steve Sax's jersey number in Tee Ball. I wanted to someday wear the blue and white of the Dodgers and play ball at Chavez Ravine.

I had the same infatuation with major league baseball and the same dreams as so many kids—mostly boys. The difference is that for little boys, the dream of playing for the Dodgers holds at least a kernel of reality. Sure, for most it's a long shot to make it to the major leagues. But maybe they could do it.

Not me. I eventually had to admit that the dream of playing for the Dodgers wasn't realistic for a girl.

The problem was I didn't have anything to replace that dream. I didn't even know much about college softball—when I was growing up there weren't even any games on TV. Softball wasn't yet in the Olympics. I couldn't see any real-life role models when I turned on the television. I didn't have any tangible goals. I loved playing softball, but I didn't really have a particular goal.

Until I got older. Letters started arriving. And I saw what was possible.

"How long should you try? Until."
—John Maxwell, leadership expert

College softball became a goal. It became a motivating factor—something that I thought of when I was exhausted from a workout or skipping a friend's party because of a game or getting up early when I was *so* tired. It helped make the sacrifices easier to handle.

My parents encouraged my dreams. My dad let me skip school every year to watch a big collegiate softball tournament that was held near our home. That kept my inner fire burning!

I started to realize what other opportunities were out there. Playing for the USA national team became a goal. And then, during the 1996 Olympics in Atlanta when the U.S. team won the first gold medal ever awarded to softball, playing in the Olympics became another huge goal.

I know how fortunate I am that I achieved many of my goals and dreams. And even some things I didn't even know were goals, such as being able to play professional softball in a women's league.

And in a roundabout way I even got to fulfill my Dodgers dream. When I was working for *This Week in Baseball*, we filmed a segment at Dodger Stadium. I got to pitch on the Dodgers' field and struck out their catcher, Paul Lo Duca! What a dream come true!

That's why I always encourage girls to dream big and shoot for the stars. When girls or their parents doubt whether they should be making sacrifices or giving up free time, I always tell them that you never know where your dreams will take you. I'm proof of that.

REACHING YOUR GOALS

The truth is there isn't just *one* way to go about achieving those dreams and goals. Just because I did it a certain way doesn't mean that's the only way to do it. There is no cookie-cutter path that everyone must follow.

I always think of Amy Hillenbrand, who was one of our assistant coaches at the University of Arizona and was one of the greatest players in the history of the program. When she came out of high school, she went to UC Santa Barbara. But it turned out that school wasn't the right fit for her, so she transferred to the University of Arizona and

> *"Many of life's failures are people who did not realize how close they were to success when they gave up."*
> —Thomas Edison, inventor

walked on to the softball team. Amy ended up earning first a partial and then a full scholarship.

Amy became a three-time All-American and a legendary player in Wildcats history. Though she never played in the Olympics, she served on the U.S. Olympic selection committee.

"I guess the moral of the story is to follow your heart, and things tend to work out," Amy told me. "I was prepared to play and pay for school, but I was in the right place at the right time. And I worked my butt off when I got there."

Celebrating with my Wildcats team. Playing college softball became my goal.
(AP Images)

At Arizona, we almost always had a walk-on on our team or a junior college transfer. These girls had taken a different path than mine but were determined to reach the same goal: playing softball for Arizona. And I admired them for that.

You may take a different path to reach the same goal as a friend. Or you may end up at a completely different destination than your teammates and friends. You have to figure out what *your* goals are and how *you* can best reach them.

Some people love sports and have the talent to play at a high level but don't want to devote their entire college experience to playing their sport. Believe me, playing Division I ball can be almost like a full-time job! Or you might live in an area where you don't have as many playing options and may need to spend a couple of years playing at a junior college.

You need to figure out your own goals. I truly believe that if you really want to play a sport, there's going to be a place for you somewhere. Be creative and determined.

TAKING CHARGE OF THE DECISION

College coaches started scouting tournaments when I was in high school. That was pretty high stress—the coaches from the biggest and best college programs were often there on the last day of tournaments for the championship games. So that was a lot of added pressure to get to the final game. If you went home early, maybe the coach would never see you or notice you.

Now I think there's even more pressure on young athletes. Top Division I programs are starting the recruiting process when kids are still in middle school. That's amazing to me because there is still so much growing ahead for athletes of that age and still so much to learn.

The scouting process shouldn't be one-sided. It shouldn't just be coaches deciding if they're interested in *you*. You should take an active role in the process of figuring out where your sport can take you. Do your research. Be your own scout.

How do you find out what schools offer your sports or what school you might be interested in? You probably know what schools are the big, power programs in your sport. Back when I was playing softball in Southern California, the programs were UCLA, Arizona, and Washington. Every girl who plays soccer knows about North Carolina. It's the same for UConn and Stanford in basketball.

But those are only the best-known names. There are so many options to explore. What's the right place for you?

Your college experience won't just be about your sport: it will be your entire lifestyle and a starting point for your future as an adult. Look at areas of the country you want to live in, at the size of the college, and whether or not the school offers the kind of major that you're interested in pursuing. For example, if I couldn't stand the sun and warm weather, Arizona would have been a silly place to go. If you really want to go to a small intimate school, then you might not want to be looking at really big schools like UCLA or Ohio State. Do you want to stay near home or explore a new part of the world?

Your teammates, older friends, and siblings are some of the best resources. Ask them about their college experiences—what they like and what they don't, even if it is not about sports. If you know anyone playing in college, pick his or her brain. Sometimes it's the littlest things that make a huge difference. For example, Coach Candrea at Arizona always let us eat with our parents after games if they were visiting from out of town. That may seem like a small thing, but many college programs don't allow players to eat away from the team. That would have been devastating to me not to visit with my family when they had traveled to see me play.

If you want to learn more about schools offering your sport, you can go to individual school websites or conference websites. You can also go to the website of the NCAA (the National Collegiate Athletic Association, which governs many college sports) where you can pull up a list of all the different schools and the sports they offer.

"Women have to harness their power. It's just learning not to take the first no."
—Cher, actress, singer, icon

Remember there are lots of different schools and levels of competition. Within the NCAA, there are three divisions—Division I, II, and III—that represent different sizes and competitive levels. NAIA (National Association of Intercollegiate Athletics) schools tend to be smaller and also offer a great opportunity. Junior colleges are also terrific places to play sports.

If you have the chance, visit some of the schools that interest you. Work in a trip with a family vacation. Or make a point to visit schools that are near where you live. While you're visiting, try to see if the coach—or an assistant coach—is available to talk. Send them an email in advance of your visit or call. You'd be surprised how accessible coaches can be. Don't be shy! I still have to remind myself that when I want something it's okay to *ask* for it.

You can make a video (or pay someone to make one) and send it to the coach of a school you're interested in. I remember walking by assistants offices at Arizona who had stacks of videos, and they were planning on watching them all. Or you can upload one online—on a scouting website or even on YouTube—and send the link to the school you're interested in. Write letters to coaches. Let them know where you'll be playing, what your skills are. It's great preparation for looking for a job. And it's a way to get noticed.

A really fantastic way to get to know about a school—and have that school get to know about you—is to attend a sports camp or clinic there. Most schools offer summer camps run by their coaches. Because it's a relatively small setting, you can get some one-on-one coaching time with the staff. You can get a feeling for the campus, the environment, the program, and also get onto the coaching staff's radar.

Practical Information about College Sports

Types of programs: The National Collegiate Athletic Association governs many, but not all, college sports. Within the NCAA there are divisions that tend to correlate with the level of competition, the size of the school, and the institution's philosophy.

Division I: This is, for the most part, the highest competitive level. Schools are allowed to award athletic scholarships.

Division II: These schools also award athletic scholarships but compete at a lower level.

Division III: These schools are not able to award athletic scholarships.

NAIA: The schools governed by the National Association of Intercollegiate Athletics schools tend to be smaller. They can offer athletic scholarships

Junior College: Two-year colleges can also offer scholarships. Athletes can transfer to a four-year program.

Club: Many club programs are highly competitive. Some sports only have club status on campuses.

Recruiting: Some people say they're being recruited if they've had any contact with a school. But being officially recruited means that you've either taken an official visit to a school, had contact with a coach off

I know a lot of girls who went to Arizona camps and clinics and ended up playing at the school.

Introduce yourself to coaches who are at your tournaments or games. I'll admit I was too shy to do that when I was in high school, but I had friends who went right up to coaches and started conversations. Don't forget—a lot of recruiting is selling. The coaches campus, been called more than once, or signed an athletic scholarship. Being recruited does *not* mean a student will be automatically admitted to a school.

Scholarships: Some sports offer full scholarships and some offer partial scholarships. In so-called "head count" sports, one scholarship goes to one athlete. In Division I the head count sports are men's and women's basketball, football, women's volleyball, women's tennis, and women's gymnastics. In other sports, one scholarship can be divided between many athletes.

Letter of Intent: A national letter of intent allows a high school student to proclaim that he/she is committed to going to a school. Once it is signed, both the school and the student must honor it—or penalties could be enforced. A verbal commitment does not officially bind the student to the school.

Walk-ons: A walk-on is an athlete who tries out for the team without a scholarship. A walk-on may make the team, often as part of a scout team. There are many success stories of walk-on athletes who prove themselves to the coach, contribute significantly, and earn a scholarship.

The NCAA Eligibility Center: This examines both the academic credentials of students and also whether or not the athletes have done anything to trigger professionalism questions in their sport.

try to sell their programs to the athletes. And girls can learn to market themselves to coaches.

One of the things I learned from being on the reality show *The Apprentice* with Donald Trump is how important it is to ask questions. To ask for an opportunity. To network. Don't be afraid. Remember, it never hurts to ask.

MAKING THE RIGHT CHOICE

I only took two recruiting trips: one to Arizona and one to Washington. Truth is I didn't even want to go to Washington. That's how made up my mind was about playing at Arizona. Some of my teammates from my travel team, the Batbusters, were already playing for the Wildcats. I felt so comfortable with Coach Candrea, who seemed like a second dad.

I didn't want to waste precious weekends out of my senior year to go to schools that I knew I wasn't going to want to attend. It seemed like a waste of my time and their money. But I did take a recruiting trip to Washington—my mom pretty much insisted. She told me I owed it to myself in case I was having a bad day during my freshman year and started regretting my choice. She thought I should at least see another school. So I went to Washington, which was beautiful.

And one of the great bonuses of my trip to Washington was that I met a lot of other athletes, like the guys on the football team. They were so tall! For one of the first times I didn't feel freakishly tall. I called my mom and said, "You should see how tall these guys are!" I had a feeling I was going to like college.

But I still knew I wanted to go to Arizona. My comfort level was so high there, which was really important to me. It was far away—but not too far. My parents could still come to visit. I already had friends there. And I could play ball at the very highest level. I actually called my parents on the Saturday night of my Arizona visit to ask them if it was okay if I told Coach Candrea I'd made up my mind. I figured there wasn't much point in waiting.

But my choice wouldn't be the right one for everyone. Everyone has different comfort levels and needs. I've heard heartbreaking stories of girls who have signed with top schools, places they thought would

"Follow your instincts. That's where true wisdom manifests itself."
—Oprah Winfrey, entertainer and media mogul

One of the biggest honors I've ever received was when U of A retired my jersey number.

be their dream choice, and they ended up hating it, and eventually transferring.

There's no doubt that playing in the kind of program I played in is an intense experience. I was with my team from 1:00 PM to 8:30 PM virtually every day. I had classes in the morning and had to do my studying at night. I worked hard to make sure I got the grades to stay eligible. Between school and softball, it was a lot of work.

I loved being part of something so much bigger than myself, walking into the McKale Center with the other Arizona athletes and feeling like we all represented something important. My world definitely revolved around softball. And it helped me create my own community in a big, bustling university. I might have classes with 400 other students, but when I walked into the McKale Center I felt like it was my home away from home.

Some people may want their college experience to be more of a balance between athletics and academics and might not be looking for such an intense athletic experience. Some athletes might find it frustrating to sit on the bench at a really competitive program and would rather find a place where they can start. Others might feel that being part of a top program, even if they're not starting, is the way to go.

The most important thing is to listen to your heart and your gut and find the place that's the right fit for you.

THE REAL PAYOFF

There's definitely a bigger payoff to athletics than finding a way to play in college or earning a college scholarship.

Parents often ask me, "Do you think my daughter is good enough to play in college? To get a scholarship?" Sometimes they're asking me that about nine-year-olds. I want to remind them that playing sports isn't just about playing in college.

Being athletic and active is a lifelong accomplishment. The value isn't just in what uniform you may end up wearing someday or the pot of gold (in the form of an athletic scholarship) at the end of the rainbow. What's the real payoff to playing sports?

- Being healthy
- Feeling good about yourself
- Gaining confidence
- Learning teamwork
- Learning to deal with failure

> *"The measure of achievement is not winning awards. It is doing something that you appreciate, something you believe is worthwhile."*
> —Julia Child, chef

Study after study shows that girls who play sports benefit in other ways—they have higher grades and fewer behavioral problems.

You may be able to play at a high level in college or even professionally. I played for five years in the National Pro Fastpitch league. Some of my best friends, like Natasha Watley, play in a professional league in Japan.

There are also so many careers that involve sports, such as coaching, training, media, marketing.

Sports can help you no matter what your future holds. Many women who have gone on to successful careers in the corporate world have an athletic background. That doesn't surprise me at all. On the playing field, girls learn how to be leaders, to work with others, to negotiate, to perform in the clutch, to deal with failure, to manage their time well, to be confident.

The lessons that I've learned in sports help me deal with not only my career, but also my personal life as a mother, wife, daughter, and friend. They are lessons that will last a lifetime and can be applied to all parts of life.

You're not going to get an envelope on your kitchen table with that particular message.

When you're wondering, "What's the point?"

The answer is—you.

Jennie's Tips for Navigating College Athletics

1. Do your research. Figure out what kind of college you're interested in. Big or small? Near home or far away? Is the school strong in the academic areas that interest you? You want your college experience to be a good fit in every way. Also make sure you know early on what the requirements are for the kinds of schools you're interested in—don't wait until the last minute in spring of your junior year or fall of senior year of high school. You won't have enough time to get your requirements done!

2. Dream big. Ever since you were a little girl, your goal may have always been to play basketball at Tennessee. Or softball at Arizona. Maybe you grew up wearing the powder blue of North Carolina and always wanted to play soccer there. Those are great dreams that can spur you on and keep you motivated. When it comes time to choose, be open-minded and pick the best program for you.

3. Be proactive. Learn to promote yourself. Contact the coaches by email or telephone. Send a video. Let them know where you might be playing. Attend their clinics or camps if you can. Visit the school. Don't be shy!

4. Don't get discouraged. I firmly believe that there is a place to play for everyone who really wants one. There are so many options now for girls and so many different kinds of programs. Keep looking. Don't rule out walking on or going the junior college route.

5. Don't be afraid to make a change. I was raised by my parents to never quit anything that I started. And I agree with that because so many times experiences that don't seem right at the beginning end up being wonderful life-shaping events. And definitely college is a time of growing pains and adjustments. But if you've given it some time and thought and it still doesn't feel right, consider transferring or finding a place that does feel right to you.

Chapter 8

The Pressure Cooker:
Handling Pressure from Parents, Adults, and Peers

I grew up on a nice flat cul-de-sac. Perfect for roller-skating.

One sunny Southern California day, I dug my skates out of the back of my closet and took them out to the curb to do some skating with my neighbor, Tracy. But Dad stopped me with the look.

"What are you doing?" he asked. "You can't do that. Your teammates are counting on you."

Where I saw a fun pastime, he saw a broken wrist. Where I saw a sunny-day activity, he saw a dark end to my softball career. That was a big wake-up call. It was the day I felt that I wasn't just Jennie Finch anymore, but Jennie Finch, the pitcher.

Another day I came home from school and announced I was invited to go skiing at Mammoth Mountain with another friend and her family. Nope, I couldn't do that either. My teammates were all counting on me. I was the pitcher.

That was a lot of pressure for a girl to handle.

I often felt like I was under pressure growing up. Pressure to be the softball star. Pressure to be the ace. Pressure to play only one sport. Pressure to be a nice girl.

You might be under pressure, too. Pressure from your parents. Pressure from your teammates. Pressure from your peers. Pressure from your coaches. Pressure from your boyfriend.

And, like me, you probably put a lot of pressure on yourself. Sometimes it seems like too much.

PARENTAL PRESSURE

Growing up, a lot of the pressure I felt was from my dad. We had one of those stereotypical parent-athlete relationships. He was very involved in my softball career—even before it was ever a career, when it was just a fun way to pass the time.

He taught me a lot. He helped me with the game. He never let me slack off, and he always expected the best out of me. He taught me to give 100 percent every single day.

He was always on me to make sure I did my workouts. He actually refused to drive me to school until I did my exercises with the Finch Windmill—the device he invented to help keep my body balanced and my arms flexible and strong. I know why he insisted; he wanted me to get the exercise done early in the day before school and practice and homework. He knew that, in all likelihood, if I didn't do it first thing, I'd never do it.

"Sometimes the most important thing in a whole day is the rest we take between two deep breaths."
—Etty Hillesum, author

But really, what parent threatens not to take their kid to school!

When he was talking about softball, Dad would refer to me as "Jennie Finch"—even when he was talking to me. I would say, "Dad, it's me. I'm right here." He sometimes made decisions that I didn't like, such as the times we switched teams. He saw the politics involved in youth sports and how some coaches were promoting their own daughters ahead of other players or teaching players the wrong things. I didn't see all that at the time. I just wanted to be with my friends.

My father was always very clear about doing things the right way. He was very black and white—there was no gray area. Now that I'm a parent I see how important that is. If you're not clear about what's right and what's wrong, kids can get confused, try to bend the rules, or they might lack clear direction. But at the time I felt like he was being rigid and putting a lot of pressure on me.

My mom did a great job of staying neutral when it came to softball. She cheered for me but didn't expect anything of me. And she was the one I could turn to if I was frustrated with my dad. She reassured me that he just wanted what was best for me. She was the moderator, convincing me to do what my dad was asking to make life easier, or suggesting to my father that he give me a little space.

Mom even started being the team scorekeeper. It wasn't because she really wanted the job, but she did it so that on trips home in the car if my dad and I disagreed about what the count was on a certain batter, or how I got her out, my mom would pull out the scorebook and calm us down with actual facts. I still turn to Mom when I'm feeling stressed out about something—she's such a rock and so matter-of-fact about how to tackle a problem.

The pressure I felt was pretty intense. It wasn't that my dad wanted to have a star daughter or that he was living vicariously through me. It's simply that he had a lot of belief in me. He saw that I had a special gift, and he wanted me to fulfill my potential. Where I felt pressure, he saw encouragement.

I know that some kids rebel against that kind of pressure. And when I was a teenager and started to want to do things other than softball, I could get upset. I would get so mad. I felt like Dad didn't care about me as a person. He took a lot of anger and frustration from me. I would storm off into my room, crying, and then pray to God that I could live a "normal" life.

Now that I'm an adult, I see things in a very different light. I know that my father could see the big picture; he knew that skipping a sleepover wasn't going to be devastating in the long run and that there was something special happening in my life with softball. I can see things for my son that he can't understand for himself. That's easier to accept when you're very small than when you're a teenager and think you know everything.

Some kids quit their sport completely because they feel so much pressure from their parents. I had a friend in junior high who was a really good player, but she quit because her home life revolved around softball. She still loved the sport, but her parents didn't give her room to breathe. It was all softball, all the time.

My dad never took it that far. He kept it in perspective. I might have threatened to quit, but I never came close to actually doing it because I really loved softball and my parents knew it. I was as driven to succeed as my dad—we're very much alike. We're both competitive and focused, which is probably why we clashed at times. But he knew how to get the best out of me. Sure, he pushed me, but he knew how far to go and when to back off.

PARENTAL SUPPORT

When I was younger I felt pressure. But I also knew I had my parents' full support, and that was so important. I might not always have agreed with their decisions. But I always knew they loved me and were trying to do what was best for me.

I also could see everyday how committed they were to me. When I think about the hours and hours they spent taking me to games,

> *"My parents are my backbone. They're the only group that will support you if you score zero or you score 40."*
> —Kobe Bryant, basketball player

sitting in the stands, schlepping me to and from practice, I'm amazed and indebted. My mother took time off of work to go to my games. My dad poured his heart and soul into softball. They never brought up the expense of my sport—even though I know it must have been significant. Just the gas alone to get to and from tournaments must have been a big deal. But I never felt that burden.

I cherished our time together, and now that I'm a mom I wonder, *Could I be so selfless and give up all my weekends and all my free time to do the same thing?*

Even now that I'm an adult, I'm so grateful to my parents for their support and generosity. They have helped me every step of the way with Ace. When I was getting ready for the Beijing Olympics and the team was crisscrossing the country on a "Bound 4 Beijing" tour, my parents and other family members caravanned behind the bus in an RV driven by my aunt and uncle, helping with not only my son but my teammate's babies, as well. I am so lucky for their incredible support.

Parents want the very best for their children, and they want them to do their very best. That can feel like pressure to a kid. If a parent says, "You can do it," sometimes the child hears, "You must do it."

The reality was my parents were also my backbone, my foundation, my driving force. My dad and I had a very close relationship. When I was young, he was home with me, while my mother worked full time. Dad packed my lunches. Dad braided my hair. Dad brought me the math book I'd forgotten at home. I spent so much more time with my father than most girls my age did. Their dads were at work. My dad was with me.

My parents, Doug and Bev, have always been my incredible support system.

It was Dad who took me to softball practice, played catch with me, helped me learn how to pitch, and who watched closely as I progressed in my sport. He was the one who could make me laugh when I was feeling down.

He had so much confidence in me that I had confidence in myself. Just like at the national championships when I was 12, he helped me find my inner strength. When he said, "You can do it," sure, I might have sometimes felt like he was *making* me do something. But really, he was encouraging me. I almost always found out that he was right: I *could* do it.

He was always there when things got tough. When coaches were unsupportive and said I didn't have what it took to be a championship pitcher. When anonymous girls left nasty phone messages on our family answering machine.

My dad was there when mean parents would yell from the stands, "She's too big. Check her birth certificate!" It's amazing how harsh some adults can be in youth sports. I couldn't believe grownups would try to discount all the hard work a kid was doing. But some of them did. I heard it—and it hurt.

But I had my dad in my corner, so I could handle anything.

COACH PRESSURE

My dad wasn't the only adult from whom I felt pressure. I felt it from other coaches. I remember my softball coaches being alarmed that I was playing volleyball and basketball in high school. Why would I do that? Why would I take time away from my "real" sport, risk an injury, and distract my focus?

I know a lot of young athletes feel pressure to specialize. I can't speak for everyone, but I know that—for me—playing those other sports was a great experience. I had been so focused for so many years on softball that it was wonderful to test myself in a different way, to use different muscles and reactions and explore a different side of my athletic ability.

Those other sports helped me become more body aware—more agile and balanced. At that point, by the time I was in high school, I was caught up in the college scholarship whirlwind. Travel ball was super intense. So playing basketball and volleyball was such a blast. It was a wonderful way to stay in shape without some of the pressure of my "real" sport.

"A coach is someone who can give correction without causing resentment."
–John Wooden, legendary basketball coach

Some people advised me not to play high school basketball, but playing made me a better athlete.

Of course, when I severely sprained my ankle playing basketball my senior year and had to tell Coach Candrea at the University of Arizona—where I had already committed to play—it made me really nervous. But to his credit, he didn't get mad. And thankfully, it wasn't a serious injury.

I also played softball in high school. While that might seem unremarkable to many people—of course a softball player would play high school softball!—in the area where I grew up, some of the kids on the top travel teams didn't play for their schools. The college coaches were scouting the travel teams. That's where the top competition was. A lot of players skipped high school softball, sometimes at the strong suggestion of their travel team coaches.

I didn't want to do that. I wanted to play high school ball and represent my school. But it was tough; in four years I had four different high school coaches. That meant every year a new coach would come in without knowing anything about the team. It would take until the end of the season for the coach to figure out the personalities and abilities of the players, and then the coach would be gone! Every year, a new coach brought in a new style of coaching— and not all of it was great.

By that time I had a lot of experience with softball coaches and had an idea of what worked and what didn't. So it was awkward for me when coaches arrived without a lot of experience. I was a student. I didn't want to correct my coach. I wanted to be respectful. Some of my coaches were just out of college, and I could tell they felt a little threatened by me—especially when they found out I was being recruited by Arizona. They put pressure on me to carry the team, but they also seemed to resent me at the same time.

There were times I wanted to quit because it was uncomfortable. But I didn't. For one thing, my parents didn't allow me to quit something I had already started. They believed in following through with your commitments. I also didn't want to let my teammates down. I had made a commitment to them.

John Wooden's Pyramid of Success

There is no secret formula for success, though I know parents and children are often searching for one. Parents wonder, "If I push harder, will my child be that much better?" Their kids end up feeling nothing but pressure.

One of my favorite formulas for success is John Wooden's Pyramid of Success. This formula isn't about winning or losing or the number of hours you practice; it's about being a complete, well-balanced person.

The late John Wooden was one of the greatest coaches in history. He came up with the pyramid during his long basketball coaching career, and his success at UCLA made people clamor for his secret.

He constructed a pyramid: the cornerstones are industriousness and enthusiasm. The rest of the foundation level includes friendship, loyalty, and cooperation.

The anchor blocks of the second tier are self-control and intentness. Coach Wooden also includes alertness and initiative.

At the heart of the pyramid—the middle level—are the attributes condition, skill, and team spirit. Rising out of those qualities are poise and confidence. And at the very top of the pyramid is the quality that we strive for: competitive greatness. He ties the pyramid together with other important attributes such as honesty, integrity, reliability, forcefulness, and faith.

Coach Wooden's point of the pyramid is that each of the blocks builds upon the level below and the starting points are basic, easily attainable human qualities. Without the foundation blocks—without each level—competitive greatness is unattainable.

His pyramid of success isn't just a tool for sports, but one for life.

High school softball was fun. It was more relaxed. Putting on the school colors was awesome. I tried to look at the positives instead of dwelling on some of my negative feelings about the coaches. There are going to be tough times—you've just got to fight through them.

It seemed like every adult I met—my coaches, other parents, my own parents—had an idea about what was best for me. By nature, I'm a people-pleaser and don't like to rock the boat. But I had to make sure I paid attention to my own feelings. Looking back, I'm grateful for having so many different coaches. I learned a lot from them—the good and the bad.

PEER PRESSURE

I was lucky in high school. I was kind of immune to peer pressure. Maybe because I was expecting so much out of myself, or maybe because I had such a strong group of good friends that I could rely on.

My closest friends were all from church-going families and shared the same values. We were all pretty straight. We would go to parties with the "popular" crowd, but none of us drank or smoked. We were all athletes and cared about our bodies; plus we just weren't interested in that stuff. When we got home really late it was because we had been at Denny's eating ice cream sundaes.

I think finding friends who are trustworthy and share your values is the best defense against peer pressure. Your gut will tell you what's right from wrong, and you should never feel pressured into behavior that feels wrong.

But sometimes peer pressure can actually be a good thing. Along with accountability, I felt peer pressure from my girlfriends in the Bomb Squad to do better academically. They were all so smart and got such good grades that I pushed myself to keep up with them.

I also had very high expectations of myself. I wanted to succeed. I wanted to make my parents and my brothers proud of me. I wanted

> *"The only pressure I'm under is the pressure I've put on myself."*
> —Mark Messier, hockey great

to stay true to my faith. I wanted to realize all my dreams and goals. I stayed focused on those things.

HANDLING PRESSURE

You might feel overloaded from stress and pressure. So how do you keep from exploding?

Realize that there are two types of pressure. There's the good kind of pressure—when your parents have high expectations for you. It's because they believe in you and want you to succeed. Think how much worse the alternative would be if no one cared about you or what you were doing!

Another good kind of pressure is the kind I felt when my girlfriends were succeeding academically and I pushed myself to keep up. Without them, I might have slacked off.

But there is also bad pressure that just makes you doubt yourself or feel stressed out. The best thing you can do is try to ignore it—growing a thick skin is very useful as is not being overly sensitive to every perceived criticism. Talk about your feelings honestly with your friends and family. And focus on the great things you have going on in your life.

Find something to laugh about every day. Nothing relieves pressure like laughter!

> *"Laughter is an instant vacation."*
> —Milton Berle, legendary comedian

Jennie's Tips for Parents

1. Know your child. Not every child responds to the same type of pressure. Know when to back off and when to push. Know when to be quiet and just give them a hug.

2. Talk to your child. Find out what she is feeling and what's happening in her life. Hear what she's saying.

3. Compliment your children when they do well! Give them hugs and kisses. And don't harp on their mistakes—they know when they've struggled.

4. Use humor. If something didn't go well, joke about it. It's a good way to teach your kids how to cope with the tough parts of life.

5. Set a good example. Don't scream or yell at games or at coaches or at other players. Be a good sport.

Chapter 9

Mental Preparation:
Your Mind Is Your
Most Important Muscle

During my softball career, I heard a lot of statistics about myself. How tall I was. How hard I threw the ball. How many wins I had. How many batters I struck out. How many shutouts I'd pitched.

But I didn't hear much about what I thought was the most important tool I had—a strong mind.

In athletics, people put too much emphasis on the body and pay too little attention to the mental part of the game. Sports taught me how to work out my mind "muscle," making it strong and focused. I learned lessons about confidence and positive thinking and the importance of preparation.

The lessons I learned in softball applied directly to the rest of my life: to school, work, and relationships.

Success in every area starts with your mental preparation.

CONTROL THE CONTROLLABLES

I can make an almost endless list of all the things I can't control when I'm pitching: the weather, the umpires, the other team, the coaches, the crowd, my teammates, the field. I could probably give you a million more.

In contrast, there is a very short list of what I *can* control: my attitude and my effort.

So if I could give only one piece of advice to girls—and this isn't just for athletes—it would be this: control the controllables.

Sometimes you probably feel like you can't control your attitude—you didn't get enough sleep, or your brother was mean to you, or your friends are being exclusive. You're in a bad mood. I know that being a young woman can be super-emotional at times.

But in reality, you can control your attitude. You don't have to let other people dictate how you should feel or bring you down. Find something positive to focus on. Don't get angry. I believe that once you're angry, you're conquered. You've given other people the power to control your feelings.

A great skill, in sports and in life, is to learn to let things roll off your back. Instead of getting upset, ask yourself whether you have any control over a situation. If you don't, then don't worry about it.

Just worry about controlling your own attitude and effort.

If you give everything you have in practice or in a game, then you're going to be able to look in the mirror and feel good about yourself. My father always urged me to give 100 percent. He stressed that it was my responsibility to both myself and my teammates.

Your effort on a daily basis directly translates into results at crunch time.

"Practice isn't the thing you do once you're good. It's the thing you do that makes you good."
—Malcolm Gladwell, writer

I made the USA National team thanks to lots of preparation. (AP Images)

Your effort influences both your attitude and your level of confidence.

If you have a big test in school and you're not prepared, do you have any confidence? Do you have a positive attitude? Nope—not if you haven't studied. But if you have a big test and you've been studying, taking practice tests, and preparing the way you should, you feel confident. You're ready to take the test.

It's the same in sports. It's important to be prepared and come with a good attitude and maximum effort.

"You can't turn it on and off like a faucet. I couldn't dog it during practice and then, when I needed that extra push late in the game, expect it to be there."
—Michael Jordan, basketball player

PRACTICE LIKE IT'S COMPETITION, COMPETE LIKE IT'S PRACTICE

This is another one of my favorite pieces of advice.

You can't train one way and then expect to jump up to another level at game time. Practice is for going all-out, training your body how to respond, pushing yourself to the limit, and getting your mind ready. Like Michael Jordan, arguably the greatest basketball player in history, said—you can't just turn it on and off.

Some people view practice as a time to take it easy. There's not going to be a result at the end of practice, no W or L, so it doesn't really count, right?

Wrong.

You have to find it within yourself—even when you don't feel like it—to practice with the same intensity and determination that you apply to game situations.

Game pressure does get intense. That's where the "compete like it's practice" part comes in—when the heat is on, you can't let yourself get too overwhelmed. You need to try to slow down the game, and just let yourself do what you've trained to do. It's a little bit of a mental trick, and the mind is the most powerful tool you have.

I've had teammates who were awesome in practice—they looked like the most supremely talented players of all time. And then they would just crumble at game time. They would collapse when the pressure got too intense. It was definitely a mental issue because physically they were being asked to do the same thing that they had done so effortlessly in practice.

The same kind of mental preparation applies in any area of life: school tests, drama performances, and job interviews. Do the hard work beforehand. Try to relax and be confident in the moment.

If you've prepared the correct way, not only physically but mentally, you have to trust it. Go for it! Bring it!

THE POWER OF POSITIVE THINKING

So much of sports is mental. If you go to the plate thinking, "Gee, I hope I don't strike out," you're already contemplating failure instead of preparing for success. When I hear people yell from the stands, "Hey, don't walk that girl," what am I suddenly thinking about? Walking the batter. Exactly what I shouldn't be thinking about.

I try very hard to shut out negative thoughts and feedback, whether I'm on the field or going through my daily life. I get sad when I hear girls say negative things about themselves—and that happens so much in middle school and high school. Girls can be really hard on themselves, and a negative mindset can just keep fueling more negativity.

There is a big difference between women and men. I think it's hard for girls to say, "I'm good at this." "I'm excellent." "I'm smart." Girls often deflect praise or attribute their success to luck or their teammates. It's important—in sports and in life—to recognize what you're good at and build confidence from those abilities.

I always tried to let my game speak for itself. I never went around saying, "I'm awesome," or "I'm dominant." Some of my teammates actually did say things like that, because they needed to say it out loud to make it a reality and that was good for them. We all find what works for us. I needed to say it in my head. I worked to be confident on the inside—if I had doubts about my ability rattling around in my mind, I would have been toast. It's a constant battle against negative thoughts.

On Fear of Failure

Overcoming a fear of failure is an important part of gaining mental toughness.

Fear of failure keeps too many people from taking any risks at all. Because we live in a culture with such a stigma about being a "loser," many people avoid failing by not doing. The pressure to be perfect can lead people to be cautious and prevents them from embracing the moment.

The truth is in sports—and in life—we are going to fail. There is no way around it. You can look at the most accomplished people in the world, and they've failed at something at some time. Failure is part of competition.

Of course, nobody wants to lose. But failure is an inevitable part of life and can be a very worthwhile experience. Many psychologists have studied failure and come to the conclusion that failure can have great benefits. Among the points I think are most worthwhile:

I remember my first tryout with the U.S. national team. I was only 16, and I was scared to death. I went into the game and looked at who was in the on-deck circle. Dot Richardson, only considered the greatest hitter in the game at the time and a total legend of our game. I was so nervous I felt like I was going to collapse. I threw my first pitch, and she got a hold of it and hammered it down the first-base line. It finally—after what seemed like an eternity—hooked foul. And then I settled down. I kept saying to myself, "You can do this, Jennie. You can do this."

- Failure can make an individual more motivated to succeed.
- Failure provides a real-life lesson in the wrong way to do something.
- Failure connects actions with consequences, thereby teaching lessons.
- Failure teaches important life skills such as commitment, patience, determination, and problem-solving.
- Failure teaches humility and an appreciation for success and opportunity.
- Rather than think of failing as not succeeding at a specific task, some suggest we should redefine failure to mean:
  — Not living by your values and morals.
  — Not giving your best effort.
  — Looking for the easy way out.
  — Treating others poorly or disrespectfully.

I ended up doing pretty well that day and gaining some confidence that I would eventually take with me to the next tryout. I was just doing what I'd been working hard at all my life, and it helped build my self-assurance. I could feel that my hard work was paying off. And the next time I was invited to a national team tryout, I wasn't nearly as nervous.

Positive thinking doesn't mean fooling yourself mentally. You have to be honest with yourself about what you're doing right and what you're doing wrong. My dad always gave me a reality check. When I thought I was throwing hard and he was pretty sure I wasn't, he would

*"Attitude is a little thing that
makes a big difference."*
—Winston Churchill, British prime minister and statesman

get out the radar gun to prove his point. And he was usually right. It's important to know the difference between thinking positively and denying reality.

It's also important to get through the bad days. Everyone has them now and then. Though my friends call me an eternal optimist, I'm not naïve. I know that there are going to be days when you're not feeling good or everything seems to be going wrong. I've had plenty of them myself; they are the kind of days that just seem to be under a dark cloud.

My advice on those kinds of days is to fake it 'til you make it. Carry yourself in a confident, positive way, and don't show others how you're truly feeling.

When I took the field on days when I wasn't feeling great, I didn't want to show my opponents that I was out of sorts. I tried to step into the circle with the utmost confidence, even if I was nervous or shaking in my cleats or feeling lousy. I wanted my opponent to know I was going to dominate.

You've got to just keep plugging away and tell yourself, "I can do this." Just plugging away is half the battle. As film director Woody Allen once said, "Eighty percent of success is showing up." So show up and, if you have to, fake it.

Also, don't be afraid to jump on a teammate's back. If you're struggling and your teammate is doing well, don't sulk. Instead, draft off her positive energy. Congratulate your teammates. Give them high fives. Positive vibes can be so contagious! It's the same idea as making sure you surround yourself with the right kind of friends. Hanging out with positive, successful people will make you feel good—in the dugout or in life.

The power of positive thinking has helped get me through the tough times. (AP Images)

Softball is a game of failure. Even the elite players fail seven out of every 10 times they come to the plate. That means even the great players experience twice as much failure as success. You have to be resilient and mentally tough enough to overcome that constant failure, to not give in to it, and to be confident that things are going to change. Overcoming mistakes and setbacks only makes you stronger.

Sure, I'm talking about softball. But I could be talking about any part of life. Look at the positive side of things, and don't give in to the negative. Life is too short.

The "fake it 'til you make it" rule works in all areas of your life. If you're in a social situation that isn't comfortable or you're feeling awkward, dig deep and find some inner confidence. Act like you're having a great time. Tell yourself that you are. Keep plugging away, and pretty soon you'll find that you don't have to fake it anymore.

GET YOUR MIND RIGHT

When I was at Arizona, we had a sports psychologist talk to us. The psychologist put a tiny toilet in the dugout. I'm not kidding.

When we would strikeout at the plate, or when a pitcher would give up a run, the psychologist wanted us to flush the tiny toilet. That was supposed to symbolize flushing the past away, getting rid of whatever bad just happened, letting it go.

Me? Sometimes I felt like smashing the tiny toilet.

Okay, so I wasn't being a very good patient for our sports psychologist. I know he was only trying to help our team. But I was so competitive that when things went wrong in a game, I was ticked off. That anger helped fuel me—it was like a fire that burned in me until I got back on the mound or until my next time at-bat. It's a different kind of anger than being angry about something you can't control. I felt I could control how I played, and any kind of failure only pushed me harder.

Every player is motivated in a different way, just like Pete Rose said. There isn't one mental approach that works for everyone. Mentally, I'm pretty hardheaded, so I wasn't receptive to some sports psychology. But there are some basic principals that worked for me.

Visualize: I didn't ever adopt specific visualization techniques. But I would go through the upcoming batters in my head and make mental notes of how I was going to pitch to each one. Before each pitch I would visualize where I wanted it to go, the spot on my catcher's mitt I wanted it to end up, and how I wanted it to break.

This probably made up for my lack of film-study when I was younger. I know some athletes swear by video preparation, and we always used film on the national team. To be honest, it sometimes just made me more nervous. If I watched video of some girl ripping a three-run homer, I had a hard time getting that image out of my head. So I guess my lack of film study was kind of an anti-visualization technique. I tried to focus more on my strengths and the hitter's weakness instead of the other way around.

Set goals: Although I didn't know that this was a big part of sports psychology when I was growing up, it's something I did all my life. When I was young, I decided I wanted to be in the Olympics. When I was at Arizona, I wanted to win a national championship. I wanted to make the USA national team. I had big goals I was striving for and little goals—like becoming the No. 1 pitcher, or beating ASU every year—that kept me focused and challenged.

"Some players you pat their butts, some players you kick their butts, some players you leave alone."
—Pete Rose, baseball player and manager

Some sports psychologists warn against setting unrealistic goals. I don't know about that. I set some pretty big goals for myself, ones that a lot of people might have called unrealistic. And many of them came true. I'm a huge proponent of dreaming big!

Stick to a routine: I definitely always tried to do this. I'm a fan of consistency. When I was young, my parents helped me stick to a pregame routine, making sure I went to bed at the right time and that I had the right food before playing. When I was on my own, I settled into my own routines like chilling out in my room before games and making sure I didn't stay out late the night before. Routine makes me feel in control and calm, giving me and my team the best chance to succeed.

Superstitions are part of routine. And I guess I was superstitious. I always had to have my lucky glitter hairband and usually a ribbon. But you don't want to be a slave to superstitions and let something throw you off mentally because you don't have the right socks or your lucky sports bra. There's a clear line between sticking with routine and investing too much power in routine.

Encourage yourself: Tell yourself, "I can do this." Point out to yourself what you're doing right. Be aware of your own strengths and don't downplay them. They are the foundations of your confidence. You have to believe!

Conversely, berating yourself usually doesn't help. I've had teammates yell at themselves or call themselves stupid. They're getting hung up on their past mistake and not concentrating on the moment. If you do yell at yourself just make sure it's in your head. Always try to be a team player and do and say what is *best* for the team. I say—and said—a lot of stuff in my head.

Control your nerves: I call this getting your butterflies to fly in formation. I don't mind having butterflies. I just want them to be under control—to have an excited, ready kind of nervousness, not a shaky, out-of-control type. I want to use my nervous energy to excel.

You can calm yourself down with deep breathing techniques, sitting quietly, and positive imagery. But the very best way to get your butterflies to fly in formation is to prepare effectively. Preparation builds confidence and pushes away self-doubt.

THE MIND IS A MUSCLE

Your mind is the strongest, most powerful muscle you have. Work it out through practice, preparation, and repetition. Preparation builds self-confidence and belief in your self. Practice helps you get rid of self-doubt and negative thoughts.

The same mental tools that help you in sports will help you in school, in your career choice, and in your interactions with others. Remember, you're developing a work ethic and mental mindset that will stay with you throughout life.

Jennie's Tips for Being Mentally Tough

1. Control the controllables. Don't worry about all the things you can't control. Work hard on your own attitude and effort.

2. Practice hard! Do everything you can to prepare and be ready. Prepare wisely. Have fun, but know that practice is for preparation.

3. Play relaxed. Don't get overwhelmed by the moment. If you've prepared correctly, you know you're ready.

4. Think positive thoughts. Push the negatives out of your mind and remind yourself of your strengths and ability.

5. Catch onto a teammate's or a friend's positive energy. If you're not having a great day, don't wallow in your own problems. Get positive energy from people who are having a good day.

6. And encourage others even when you are at your worst! Fill other people's buckets up with encouragement and eventually it will overflow into yours. The more you encourage others the better you will feel.

III. HEART

Chapter 10

The Team:
Leadership, Great Teammates, and Not So Great

When I was at the 2008 Olympics in Beijing, I watched almost every one of Michael Phelps' races. It was incredibly compelling to watch the great American swimmer on his quest for eight individual gold medals. Although I was in Beijing, because of our training schedule I couldn't get to the Water Cube to watch him. Instead, my teammates and I would gather at the Athletes' Village to watch him race.

He kept winning, race after race, gold medal upon gold medal. It was amazing. And at the end of every race he would raise his fists and celebrate—by himself.

To me, the most amazing part of his accomplishment was that he was doing it alone in an individual sport. He had to get up at dawn and swim laps alone. He had to push himself. He had to rely on his inner strength. As I sat there watching him, surrounded by my teammates, I wondered if I could have that kind of strength.

When my team won on the softball field, we jumped up and down together. We dogpiled on top of each other. We hugged and laughed and cried together. When I had to get up to run early in the morning, my teammates were there with me. When I cried after a loss, my teammates were with me. When I shouted with joy over a gold medal, my teammates were with me. Being on a team was a shared journey.

While I have all the admiration in the world for individual sports and their athletes, I can't tell you how much I love being on a team. Having a teammate's back, knowing that they have my back. Sharing the field with women who know exactly how much that one loss hurt, just how great that big win was, and why that ridiculous joke was so funny.

There's a bond and a sisterhood that's unlike anything else I've ever experienced. And like any sisterhood, it has the good, the bad, and the ugly. We spent as much time together—if not more—than normal sisters do. I always tried my best to be a good teammate. And I've had some incredible teammates over the years.

TEAMMATES AND LEADERS

When I think about great teammates, I think about Teresa Ayoub.

On our national championship team at Arizona, Teresa didn't play much. In fact, she only pitched two innings that entire year. But I think every player on that special team would call her our most important teammate.

She brought so much to our team chemistry in terms of work ethic and attitude. And she brought it all from a place where a lot of players pout or grumble. She brought it from the bench. And the heart.

Teresa provided a great lesson in leadership. A leader doesn't have to be the star of the team or the most statistically impressive player. Leadership can come in many different ways. Leaders can be vocal. Or

> *"Ask not what your teammates can do for you. Ask what you can do for your teammates."*
> —Magic Johnson, basketball Hall of Famer

they lead primarily by example. Leaders can be beloved. Or they can even be abrasive at times. It all depends on the makeup of the team.

But I believe you have to know your role. You can't join a team and start bossing people around without any authority. It's important to be respected as someone who has enough experience and understanding that your opinions and guidance are valued.

Being a leader is sometimes hard work. It's not always a popularity contest. When I was a senior at Arizona, some freshmen came up to me at the end of the season and thanked me for being so hard on them at times. I had only wanted to encourage them to be the very best they could be. But when I had given them advice, they hadn't liked it—and they hadn't liked me very much. But after going through a full collegiate season, they realized that what I had told them was worthwhile.

One of the best teammates I ever had is Lisa Fernandez, who I consider the greatest player our game has ever seen. She was my idol when I was a girl, and I was fortunate to become her teammate on the U.S. national team. She brought so much intensity to practice and games every single day. If you had a weakness, she would let you know about it.

I know that some of my other teammates felt threatened by Lisa or couldn't handle her directness. But I loved and admired her for it. I think every team needs someone like that—the enforcer, the person who keeps everyone honest and in check. Not only would she do her best to make sure we didn't have any weaknesses, but we all knew that she would be completely prepared in every aspect of her own game. Lisa was tough, but all she wanted was for us to be successful as a unit.

There's nothing like the sisterhood of playing on a team. (AP Images)

Are team captains important? It is certainly an honor to be a captain. And it is necessary to have someone who can communicate between the players and the coach and vice versa—a person who can keep communication going in both directions and within the team.

But I honestly don't know if captains are really necessary. The true team leaders will be revealed naturally and will become the real captains, whether or not they're wearing an armband or given a title. I think when a coach appoints a team captain it can sometimes make a situation more difficult. The person may not have earned that credibility within the team or may be viewed as the coach's pet.

Sometimes on new teams, it's hard to know who the leaders are, so a coach will name someone based on seniority or experience or attitude. But eventually, the true leaders will surface. And they might not always be the people you would expect or in the roles you would predict.

LEADING BY EXAMPLE

My view of leadership was to keep things simple. No big speeches or drama. A simple word to a teammate. A high-five coming off the field.

How can you lead by example? By being the hardest worker possible. By having a positive attitude. I hope that those two attributes—effort and attitude—helped me earn my teammates' respect and my role as a leader.

As I got older and more veteran on whatever team I was on—from high school to college to the national team—I felt more comfortable being assertive and being a vocal leader. When I felt I needed to speak up, I did. I would sometimes have to say something to my teammates on the field about picking up their effort. But I always tried to make sure to say it in an encouraging way and to make sure that my own effort was always at 100 percent. There's nothing worse than someone who doesn't walk her own talk.

I remember once in college, a teammate was slacking on the toughest day of preseason conditioning. We had to do sprints. The coaches trusted us to be responsible—they weren't watching us every second. (That was something I found surprising when I first got to college!) One girl told the coaches she'd done the entire workout, but the rest of us knew she had skipped it. We knew that if we told on her, we'd all be punished, and the entire team would have to run more sprints because of her laziness.

But if we didn't inform the coaches, she would have known that we let her get away with cutting corners. That we weren't holding her accountable to the team. By not speaking up, it would imply we were okay with people who took shortcuts or cheated.

So guess what our decision was? Yep, we told the coaches that she hadn't done the work that all the rest of us had done. We all had to run because of it. And remember—this was in the Arizona desert! It was hot. It was miserable. But the message was sent and received. We were all accountable to each other. It was an important part of team building.

That was something we could control. We had to make a choice— were we willing to pay the price to bring someone else in line? There are other things you can't control. For example, I couldn't control whether my teammates wanted to lie by the pool all day before a game. Personally, I wanted to relax inside and stay cool and focused. But that was my choice. I had to trust that my bronzed teammates would be ready to go when game time came. There may have been times when they wondered about my commitment.

Even at the Beijing Olympics, one of my teammates came into my room before the gold medal game and asked about some corporate party

"I am a member of a team and I rely on the team, I defer to it and sacrifice for it. Because the team, not the individual, is the ultimate champion."
—Mia Hamm, soccer player

that was supposed to take place later that night. I was baffled. How could she be thinking about that before the biggest game of our lives?

I checked the impulse to explode and just reminded her that we had a game to play and could talk about other things later. I can't get angry that my teammates don't approach every game the same way I do. We're all wired differently. My biggest concern was always that we were all on the same page at game time.

DEALING WITH DIFFICULT TEAMMATES

I feel blessed to have been on some great teams. After the Athens Olympics, *Sports Illustrated* even anointed our team "The Real Dream Team" on its cover. Like so many other great teams—the 1999 U.S. World Cup team, the 1996 U.S. gymnastics team—we had terrific chemistry and cohesion.

I wish that kind of cooperation and teamwork could become the norm. Instead, all too often, women have to put up with the *Mean Girls* image and the assumption that girls will stab each other in the back and be separated by petty jealousies.

Still, the *Mean Girls* stereotype definitely is based in reality. Trust me, I know all about the drama.

I've been burned by mean girls. When I was a freshman in high school, a sophomore went around telling the other softball players that I was a stuck-up snob. I only found out because the seniors came to me and said, "Hey, so-and-so told us you were so full of yourself. And you're actually not like that at all."

I was devastated. I didn't even really know the other girl. Why was she saying things about me behind my back? I was just a dorky freshman. The last thing I felt was full of myself. It ate me up inside that someone could be so mean.

Looking back I can see that the girl was threatened—I had a reputation as a good player that I'd earned from travel ball. I played her position. She was insecure and wanted to bring me down, and

The Bomb Squad was my off field team and support group.

she did to some extent. It was so hard playing beside someone who betrayed you.

But understanding her motives didn't make it hurt any less. I was too much of a chicken and felt like I was too young to confront her at that point. Ultimately, I became friends with the seniors while she was on the outside. She created dissension, and it came back to hurt not me, but her. In my experience, that often happens. People reveal their true colors, and if they are mean to others, eventually people don't want to be friends with them.

When I had a similar experience in college, I had to deal with it in a different way. Once again, a teammate said that I was all about myself, that all I cared about was modeling and my career after softball—which was so far from the truth. The only thing on my mind was winning another national championship. And once again, I found out from some other girls. I felt so betrayed and hurt.

However, we were going to be teammates for a while. I could tell my feelings were affecting me. So I learned to forgive her and moved on, and over time, our relationship got a little bit better. I didn't want to have a toxic environment every time we were together, so I had to free myself from all the negative feelings. Of course, that's easier said than done. I worked hard not to dwell on negative feelings.

Should you confront a teammate? I know that's a really hard thing to do. It affects you beyond just the playing field. You probably have to be with that girl at school all day. You have mutual friends. And while it can feel good to get things off your chest and talk about your troubles, sometimes—especially with girls—the more you talk about something the bigger an issue it becomes. If you talk to one girl, pretty soon everyone will find out what you were saying—no matter if you've sworn your friend to secrecy. Little rifts can become big ones that can consume a team.

But teams have to work together. I think girls' teams, even more than boys' teams, are based on communication and interpersonal relationships. You don't have to be best friends with everyone. You don't even have to like everyone. But you need to respect your

"Remember not only to say the right thing in the right place, but far more difficult still, to leave unsaid the wrong thing at the tempting moment."
—Benjamin Franklin, American statesman

Chemistry

Team chemistry is a chicken-and-egg question in sports. What comes first? The great chemistry between the players, which leads to winning? Or does winning create good chemistry?

There are a lot of different opinions on the subject. I know that on the best teams I was on, the chemistry was good. Everyone was working together for the same goal. But those teams were also some of the most successful teams I've ever been on. Winning helps to get everyone on the same page. So it is difficult to separate the winning from the good chemistry when people put themselves second and the team first.

Teams at every level try to unlock the magic of great chemistry. The winner of the 2010 World Series was an interesting examination of team chemistry. The San Francisco Giants surprised baseball by winning the World Series. They were an unusual team because they had been put together on the fly, midway through the season, with players who had been dropped by other teams and call-ups from the minor leagues. The team didn't start winning until all the pieces had been assembled.

Bruce Bochy, the Giants manager, said the chemistry was as good as on any team he's managed. "They've coalesced into a bunch of guys that have one agenda, and that's to win and get to the postseason," he said. "They do a great job of holding each other accountable and playing the game right and playing the game hard.... They came in prepared every day."

The Giants didn't have a star. They had a mixture of veterans and rookies, players who had been around for years and some who had only been there a few weeks. And they got contributions out of almost every player.

That team is one example where the chemistry seemed to happen naturally. And the winning followed.

teammates, get along, and be able to work together. Coach Candrea always said that girls have to feel good to play good. Guys are a little different. Guys can duke out and the next minute be friends. Girls—we tend to hold it all in, and it usually builds and ends up blowing up into something big.

If your experience isn't fun, you're going to want to quit. So sometimes—rather than quit to avoid confrontation and therefore rob yourself of the joy of playing—you have to take the uncomfortable step of talking to someone directly about a problem.

My recommendation for dealing with a difficult teammate is to approach her one-on-one, away from the team, and voice your concerns, especially if the issue is between the two of you. If you stay silent, it just implies that you're on board with her behavior or that you don't care.

But if that one-on-one interaction doesn't resolve things, you can try talking in a team setting. You don't want someone to feel like she's under attack or that everyone is ganging up on her. But the girl who is an issue probably needs to know that her actions and words impact the team. The message can be simple, "We're a team. Let's deal with this issue together." Some people might not realize how much their actions or attitude can affect everyone around them. Until things are out in the open, the issue won't be resolved.

How a message is received is often in the tone and manner in which it's delivered. You don't want to accuse anyone or get her on the defensive. If you have a criticism, it's best to think of some positive things to say, too.

An example: "We love your spirit and your sense of humor. But we are concerned about _____."

Encouragement is so important, whether it's part of delivering a difficult message or just part of the overall team dynamic. I believe great team leaders encourage their teammates and praise them. When most of the message is positive, it's much easier to accept the criticism. Some experts say a 5:1 ratio is a good target—five positive comments for every critical one.

I believe that communication is vital in any well-functioning unit. Good teammates talk to each other on and off the field. Good teammates welcome newcomers. They accept their teammates' differences—whether those differences are in how they live or how they're motivated on the field.

Good teammates are unselfish. If you're having a bad day, encourage your teammates—it will ultimately make you feel better and allow you to contribute in a way other than on the field. If I didn't get a hit, I wanted nothing more than to cheer on my teammates who did. It helps you get out of your own funk and think about the team even when sometimes it's so hard—you want to contribute and if you don't, you feel like you are letting down your team. Try to "think team" in all situations.

The main reason girls play a sport is because it's fun. And teammates are a huge part of the fun and joy of playing. Being with friends, working together toward a common goal, bonding with girls you might never know otherwise, laughing together, crying together, jumping with joy together.

Really, in my opinion, those are the best parts of sports.

Jennie's Tips for Being a Good Teammate

1. Communicate. Talk is such an important part of sports—on the field, in the dugout, at practice. I don't mean long drawn-out speeches. And I don't mean constant chatter during practice. Good communication includes giving encouragement, being honest, sharing information, and cheering each other on.

2. Earn your respect and role on the team. Set a good example. Work hard. Stay positive. Be the kind of teammate you would like to have. If you don't, you have little credibility when it comes to offering advice or complaining if things don't go well.

3. Know your role. Where do you fit into the team? You probably can't come in and start telling others what to do right away, though some young players can come in and become instant team leaders because of their personality, talent, or work ethic. If you've been on a team a while, think about taking a more active leadership role. Don't always defer to others.

4. Be positive. Use the magic ratio of five positive comments for every one that might be viewed as critical. Look for the good things your teammates do. Cheer them on.

5. Embrace the sisterhood. Being on a team is a special dynamic. You'll be on other teams in your life: your family, your workplace, at school. But a sports team is a unique and special unit. Enjoy it!

Chapter 11

Inspiration:
Where to Find It,
How to Tap Into It

The sound of metal cleats click-clacking on cement.

The empty green field of Dodger Stadium.

The look on my son's face when I get home from a trip.

Those are some of my inspirations.

We all have different things that inspire and motivate us. What resonates with you might not mean a thing to your best friend. And sometimes it's the smallest things that can inspire you to push yourself.

For me, just the sound of a team of college or professional players walking across cement on their way to the field—their metal cleats click-clacking in unison—always fills me with excitement. It reminds me of being allowed to miss school when I was young in order to attend a big college softball tournament near my house. Those girls walking out to the field were living my dream. It made my goals and dreams so real and tangible. That sound can bring back the thrilling feeling that anything is possible.

Sometimes it's a big thing that inspires you, like faith in God. My faith helps me embrace every day as a gift. It helps me to know that there's a bigger picture. It gives me inner peace believing that it's not just about me and my struggles but that there's a bigger plan.

Sometimes, let's face it, we're not really inspired. We have to just lace up our shoes and get to work. But it helps to have a reservoir of inspiration that we can draw from on those days.

BIG DREAMS

Big dreams and goals can help fuel your fire. My first inspiration came from watching the Los Angeles Dodgers. I wanted to wear that Dodger blue. I wanted to play on that perfect green diamond. I wanted to be Orel Hershiser.

When I watched the Olympics I was inspired. To see the athletes march in to the opening ceremonies. To see the medal ceremonies and hear "The Star-Spangled Banner" being played. There's a picture of me in a USA jersey from the 1984 Olympics, which were held in Los Angeles. I was only four! I don't remember much from those games, but I've felt an attachment to the Olympics my entire life. I loved watching Kristi Yamaguchi win the skating gold and following Mary Lou Retton. I always liked watching the gymnasts and skaters—the dainty, super-feminine athletes—maybe because I felt I was exactly the opposite.

I was inspired by *A League of Their Own*; I was 12 when that movie came out. I loved seeing a team of women—the Rockford Peaches—

"Are you crying? There's no crying in baseball!"
—Jimmy Dugan, *A League of Their Own*

*Even when I was four,
I was already dreaming
of the Olympics!*

doing what my teammates and I were doing. I could quote every line in that movie. It was so amazing to me that they had a league back then and we didn't have a league of our own. It really inspired me to work to make my dreams come true because I knew that it had happened before.

I tell girls to practice their autograph. Why not? It helps turn your dreams into reality. Practice how you want it to look. Add your number on the bottom. Full name or an initial and last name? Believe in yourself! Someday people will be asking you for your autograph. You have to believe. You have to make it real and know it is going to happen!

My parents encouraged me to dream big. When I was young I had a Dot Richardson bat. But when I was about 10, my dad went to a company where they would engrave my own name on the bat. So every time I came to the plate, I did it dragging along a Jennie Finch bat. And now there is a line of Mizuno Jennie Finch bats!

One of the most exciting moments in my career was when I got my first pair of metal cleats at the University of Arizona. As soon as I put them on, I started searching for cement so I could be the one making the sound that had inspired me for so many years. Our locker room was carpeted, so I went into the bathroom and tapped my feet on the tiles. I thought to myself, "I've made it! I finally have my own pair of metal cleats!" Of course my teammates were wondering, "What the heck is Jennie doing, tap-tap-tapping her feet in the bathroom?" During college, I think I must have worn out twice as many cleats as anyone else. I blamed it on my pitching toe, but really, it was probably because I liked to walk on cement whenever I could!

One of my favorite things to do is to share my Olympic medals with girls. I love to see their eyes light up when they hold them. I love to place them around their necks and let them take a picture. I want them to feel how heavy they are, how substantial and real.

My two Olympic medals are kind of beat up because I take them out to the ball field, out in the rain and the heat, to speaking engagements. Over the years, thousands of kids have handled them. My philosophy is I can't take them to the grave. The greatest thing about having the medals is to be able to share them. I want girls to be able to touch them and be touched by them. They're a symbol of realized dreams.

I hope some girl who holds my Olympic medal is inspired.

ROLE MODELS

My biggest role model growing up was Lisa Fernandez. She was playing at UCLA when I was getting serious about softball, and she led the Bruins to two national championships. She broke that stereotype that pitchers just pitch—she did it all. She was a great hitter and third baseman, and she was a phenomenal pitcher.

Lisa was from a town near mine, and since she played in Southern California, I had the chance to watch her play. We worked with some of the same coaches. I used to watch her workout beyond the fence,

> *"You just can't beat the person who never gives up."*
> —Babe Ruth, baseball Hall of Famer

completely in awe. At one game, I got the chance to be a UCLA batgirl. I was so shy! I just watched and absorbed everything she did.

My admiration for her only grew when we became teammates on the national team. One day, I saw her put on every single piece of USA softball clothing she had. All the gear possible—T-shirts, sweatshirts, fleece pullovers. It was 90 degrees outside!

"Lisa, what the heck are you doing?" I asked her.

She told me that she was trying to get herself as uncomfortable as possible. She said, "If I can be really uncomfortable and still pitch, then I know that when we're at the Olympics in Athens I'll be able to pitch."

Lisa told me that sometimes, when the sprinklers came on the field to water the grass, she went out in them and pitched. Her rationale?

"If I can pitch in sprinklers then I can pitch in rain," she said.

That was amazing to me. She pushed herself so hard that I felt I had to keep pushing harder and harder, just to be worthy of being her teammate.

She took training to a whole new level. She was, and is, a total inspiration to me.

FAMILY

My family is, by far, my biggest inspiration. I want to make them proud. I always wanted to play hard for the name—my name, their name—on the back of my jersey.

Dad has worked so hard with me. He was—and is—my rock. He expected a lot out of me, and I never, ever wanted to let him down. He let me know that whatever tough times I had, they were also life lessons.

Mom played high school softball back in Iowa. She was, I've heard, very talented. But there was nowhere to go back then. There

"Some people grumble because roses have thorns.
I am thankful that thorns have roses."
—Alphonse Karr, French novelist

were no collegiate softball programs. And never in a million years did Mom think she'd have a daughter who could play collegiate sports and compete in the Olympics. It's so inspiring to me that I *can* do all this, that I have these opportunities that generations of women before me never had.

My brothers have always been a big inspiration. They were great athletes, playing baseball and basketball. And they lit a competitive fire in me at an early age—as a little girl trying to get noticed by her two big brothers and get them to play with her, I had to be strong and assertive!

I'm so proud of them now. They both graduated from college—the first in our family to do so. They have always been such outstanding examples to me, and they have fully supported me throughout my life. It's inspiring for me to see the men, husbands, and fathers that they've become.

GUIDING LIGHTS

My grandparents were enormous inspirations to me. They were from the countryside in Iowa—my dad's parents were from Hawarden, population 2,000, and my mom's parents were from nearby Ireton, population 500. I spent a lot of time in Iowa while I was growing up, and my grandparents often came to California to see our family. Even though I grew up in the Los Angeles area, I've always felt like a Midwestern girl at heart. That's where our family's roots are, and my grandparents embodied a simple, hardworking lifestyle—they had been married for more than 50 years!

When I was about to leave for my first year of college, my grandfather passed away suddenly. He and Grandma had spent the entire summer with us, and they were driving back home to Iowa. Just a few hours from home, he had a heart attack. I went to Iowa for the funeral and then flew back home and drove to Tucson by myself to start college while my parents stayed in Iowa to be with my grandmother. When I got to my new apartment, I slept on the floor in a sleeping bag for the first couple of nights and cried myself to sleep. Instead of being an excited freshman ready to start to college, I was at one of the lowest and loneliest points in my life.

My grandfather was always so proud of me. He was the kind of guy who would meet everyone in the stands at my games and find out everybody's life story. When I came off the field, he would introduce me to all his new friends. And of course, they knew all about me—Grandpa loved to brag about his granddaughter. In their small town in Iowa, everyone knew everything about me. I was the youngest grandchild and the only girl, so he lavished attention on me. He was my No. 1 fan.

My grandmother has always been my guardian angel. She prays for us daily and just showers us with love. Even in her late eighties, she still made a point of trying to get to many of my games, even asking my uncles to drive her all the way to Oklahoma City. She got ESPN just so she could watch softball, and she has pictures of me and newspaper articles all over her house. After the 2004 Olympics, I was asked to be the Grand Marshal of the Ireton parade, and both my grandmothers rode on a fire truck in the parade. My grandma invited everyone to

"We cannot live for ourselves alone. Our lives are connected by a thousand invisible threads, and along these sympathetic fibers, our actions run as causes and return to us as results."
—Herman Melville, author

My grandmother is one of my greatest sources of inspiration.

come to her house—there were girls arriving from several towns away, coming through the farmland to get my autograph. It reminded me of *A Field of Dreams*!

It was never about softball when I was with my grandparents. They were an escape for me from everything else going on in my life. When I think of them, I feel warm and comfortable.

That first night I got to Arizona I was so sad, thinking about how lonely my grandmother must be without my grandpa and how sad I was that he would never get to see me play in college. But inside my sadness I found an inspiration to go out and represent his memory and their love as best as I can. I wanted to continue to make them both proud.

On Volunteering

One of the greatest ways to be inspired is to give back to others.

Volunteering for charities and non-profits is both humbling and motivating. It can really put things in perspective. Looking outside yourself can relieve the stress that comes from being so absorbed in your own issues.

There are so many worthwhile organizations that could use your energy and enthusiasm. One of my favorites is The Miracle League, which affords children with disabilities the chance to play baseball and softball. The Miracle League players are assisted by buddies, mainstream children who play sports or serve in community groups.

The Miracle League is just one example of the fantastic work being done in our communities. Keeping it just in the sports world, there are many worthwhile nonprofits that are reaching out to girls and young women to teach them about exercise, healthy eating, fitness, and sports.

This isn't just a movement in our country, but a global movement. More and more, there is a growing acknowledgment that sports can be a tool for empowerment for females. In countries where women don't have many opportunities—in places like the Middle East, Africa, and South America—nonprofits are using athletics as a way to get girls involved.

How can you find out about what's going on in your community? Ask around. Keep your ears open. Do a Google search. Check the website of the Women's Sports Foundation, which has a terrific GoGirlGo! program and information on other nonprofits. Some organizations run after-school programs. Others have international summer programs in other countries.

Giving back and helping other kids discover the joy of being active, using their bodies, and having fun is incredibly inspirational.

MY BOYS

I found a profound new level of inspiration when I fell in love with Casey. And then again when Ace was born.

Casey and I met in the spring of 2002 and embarked on a whirlwind romance. We had so much in common. Growing up we had made the same sacrifices for our sports. We had the same values and beliefs. It was so exciting to find someone who felt like my soul mate.

Just seven months after our first date, he blindfolded me and took me out to the pitching mound at Hillenbrand Softball Stadium at the University of Arizona. When he took the blindfold off, he was down on one knee with a ring.

"You have been the queen of the diamond for four years," he told me. "Now I want you to be the queen of my heart."

How could I say no?

But really, we were too young to get married right then. I was only 22 and Casey was only 21. I knew we were going to have a long engagement and, to be honest, it was rocky at times.

Both of our careers were taking off. He was pitching in the big leagues. I was getting a lot of notice in the aftermath of a collegiate national championship and in the lead-up to the 2004 Olympics. We were experiencing new things at the same time that we were trying to get to know each other. We had to learn to trust each other. And we had to learn to make each other priorities in our lives

It wasn't always easy going. We were so young that we didn't have a great sense of who we were. But we knew we loved each other, and that kept getting us through the tough times. Everything in our lives

"We never know the love of the parent until we become parents ourselves."
—Henry Ward Beecher, author

was a real whirlwind during those few years and, even though I have a huge fear of commitment, I learned it was incredibly comforting to be committed to someone. Casey was my one constant.

When we did get married in January 2005—making an oath under God, in front of friends and family—it was not only a great joy but also a huge relief. It was a commitment to each other, but it was bigger than that. There was less uncertainty about things. We are together, forever. That is amazingly inspirational.

And then along came Ace, and I discovered a level of love and devotion I didn't know existed. Until then I hadn't truly understood and appreciated my parents' commitment to me and their selflessness and involvement in my life. After Ace was born, I totally got it. It hit me like a ton of bricks, and I was filled with gratitude.

I found out I was pregnant in September 2005. Both Casey and my girlfriend, Jasmine, told me—at separate times within the same week—that they had dreamt that I was pregnant. I just laughed and told them they were crazy. Turns out they were right.

I was so excited at the thought of being pregnant, I took the pregnancy test right in the Walgreens bathroom. When it came out positive, my first thought was, *Oh my gosh. How am I going to pull this off?* And then I had to rush to drop off Casey at the field for work, so I was left alone with my mind spinning.

I had World Championships in China the next summer and then the build up to the Beijing Olympics. I was hoping to be a key member of the national team. I hadn't planned to have a baby in the middle of all this. But life doesn't always go according to plan. I was getting an early lesson in the main rule of motherhood: you can't control everything. And Ace was the biggest blessing above all else—even if I never threw another pitch.

My mentality during the entire was pregnancy was, "Hey, I'm going to do this." I looked to other women athletes who had managed motherhood and a playing career—women like Joy Fawcett from the

U.S. national soccer team and Leah O'Brien-Amico from our team, who had her son, Jake, between the 2000 and 2004 Olympics. They were proof that it could be done. It was refreshing to know that it was possible to be a mom and still play.

I tried to never let doubt enter my mind. I was just going to do whatever it took to be a great mom and a great softball player.

I pitched until I was six months pregnant. After that, I worked my arm and lifted weights. The national team was training in Arizona and I hung around them, eager to get back and to also let them know I was still wanting more than anything to be back. I took long walks. I had never been so sedentary in my life! I was bored. Looking back, I think that's probably the last time for a long time that I'll be bored.

Luckily, I was blessed with a pretty easy delivery. Ace was born on May 4, 2006. One look at him, and it was all over. You think you've got everything under control, and then this little guy comes along and steals your heart and every single piece of you.

I had six weeks to get back in shape for the tryouts for the World Championship team. I started working out right away. First a slow jog. Then adding on a little bit more. I started pitching and working on my arm strength, doing the Finch Windmill throughout my entire pregnancy. Casey was in the midst of his season. So two weeks after Ace was born, he and I got on a plane and flew to Los Angeles where I started training seriously and throwing with my dad.

But it was tough. My body felt different. And my heart was definitely different. It was so humbling. Having a baby put everything else in perspective.

There were some rough times. It wasn't easy. After I made the team, I came home with the schedule and burst into tears. The tears were a mixture of joy and relief at making the team but mostly tears from being overwhelmed with the schedule. There were so many games in so many places. I said to my mom, "How am I ever going to do this?" My mom was so great. She was my rock.

"Jen, we will find a way," she said. "We'll take it one trip, one day, one week at a time. We'll get through it."

When Ace came along, he stole my heart.

And sure enough, we did. That's kind of how I've approached my life ever since Ace was born—to try to live in the moment and take it one step at a time.

I spent the first three months of Ace's life on the road in Ontario, Canada; San Diego, and Oklahoma City. My mom was helping most of the way, which was a blessing. I could be myself with my mom. I could let down and cry when I needed to—which was pretty often. I tried to see Casey when possible—which wasn't very often.

The day before we were leaving for China, we were playing a game at Stanford and Ace broke out in a rash. I was so stressed out. My mom, who had worked in the NICU at a hospital for more than 30 years, was calling all the doctors she knew. I was totally second-guessing myself, wondering if I was being selfish to try to bring my little baby on the road with me.

We brought so many supplies to China: formula, diapers, every medication you could think of. It was very nerve-wracking. When we got to China everyone wanted to touch the baby. Our sleeping patterns were all messed up. It was a wild ride. Ace was still not sleeping through the night.

But we survived. After the world championships, which we won, I could relax for a few months and just stay at home with my little guy. The next year I was back at it, of course. And I found out what all working moms discover—it doesn't get any easier with time. But it also helped me realize that it *was* possible. I could do anything I set my mind to.

My first long trip away from Ace was to Brazil when he was about a year old. I was gone 15 days. I cried many times on the flight to South America. Of course, my younger teammates couldn't really understand my pain. But then one night, I Skyped with him. My mom held him by the computer, and I could see him reach toward the screen and say "ma-ma." I just lost it. And so did all of my teammates. We were all crying around my computer. I had to stop Skyping after that.

But for most of Ace's early years, he traveled with me. He was my little travel buddy. I never took a magazine or an iPod on an airplane after he was born it was just me and my boy hanging out. If my parents or in-laws weren't around, my teammates would help and hang out with us on the road. Everyone fell in love with him. They were so very sweet with him. They took him in as another teammate! He was so laid back and easy going.

Together, we made it work with an unbelievable amount of support. My parents, Casey's parents, and both of our extended families were fantastic. And Casey was terrific; he sacrificed so much. He let me go on the road with our baby. He let me be selfish—because there was no way I was going to be gone from Ace for days and days at a time.

Most baseball players want their wives in the stands supporting them. It takes away from their loneliness on the road, I think. I know that my not being there for Casey was hard for him, but he still encouraged me in my career, and I am so grateful for that.

Having Ace changed everything about my life. No more hanging out with teammates after practice, going to movies, or shopping. I rushed back to the hotel to be with Ace. No more sleeping in. I got up early to make sure I got my workouts in before Ace woke up. I became efficient and streamlined. Or, at least, I tried my best to be.

Every moment away from Ace was a huge sacrifice. I was okay when I was playing, but when I was alone—in a hotel room or on a bus—my heart was aching. Then when I'd get home there was so much to catch up on. I would be deluged with phone calls, emails, requests, and errands. I guess that's a mother's lot in life—feeling guilty that they're not doing the best job. I felt constantly torn between being the best mother, best wife, and best player/person I could be.

I hope some day Ace is able to look at my softball career and feel proud that his mom was able to do all that when he was a baby.

But even if he doesn't, I hope he always knows that he's my biggest inspiration.

Jennie's Tips for Finding Inspiration

1. Dream big! Don't let anyone tell you not to. Allow yourself to daydream and fantasize. Your goals and dreams may shift and change, but if you believe in yourself, anything is possible.

2. Surround yourself with positive images. When you see a photo that inspires you, tear it out of a magazine or print it out. Hang it on the wall. Copy down inspirational quotes and post them on your walls or inside your locker.

3. Music! Few things can be as inspirational as music. We all have our songs that excite us and empower us and just conjure up great feelings. Music can make our souls soar. Make a playlist with your favorite songs—not just pump-up songs (though those are awesome, too), but songs that inspire you.

4. Pray/reflect. Whatever your religion or faith, take some quiet time. Pray. Connect with nature. Meditate. Give thanks.

5. Set goals. Post a list of goals on your bedroom wall. Look at them every day. Revise them. Add to them. Remind yourself to dream and believe.

JENNIE FINCH'S PUMP-UP PLAYLIST

"I Gotta Feeling"—Black Eyed Peas

"Take My Life"—Jeremy Camp

"It's My Life"—Bon Jovi

"Baby I'm Ready to Go"—Republica

"Still Haven't Found What I'm Looking For"—U2

"Living on a Prayer"—Bon Jovi

"Don't Stop Believing"—Journey

Chapter 12

Pressure as a Positive:
Embrace the Heat

When I was a sophomore in college, I was battling to be my team's top pitcher.

It was the position I had strived for—to be the player my teammates trusted to have the ball in a crucial game. I was doing everything I could to earn that role and their respect.

I had come in as Arizona's top recruit. Actually, I was the only recruit that year, the one freshman on an experienced team. And I had learned quickly during my freshman year that college softball was going to be tough. Nothing was going to be handed to me just because I had been a standout player in high school.

After that first-year learning experience, I rededicated myself. I was pitching well in my sophomore year and feeling good. I was determined. And I had lost only one game all season.

In late April, we traveled about 100 miles north from Tucson to Tempe to play our archrival, Arizona State. The rivalry is so intense it splits the whole state in half. If there's one thing you learn as soon as you step on the Arizona campus and put on a Wildcats uniform is that you never, *ever* lose to ASU.

That hadn't been too much of a problem for our softball team. At that point in time, Arizona State had lost to us for 38 straight softball games. That means I had been just a kid—one who had little notion of the intensity of collegiate rivalries—the last time the Wildcats had lost to their archrival.

I was scheduled to pitch the first game of the two-game series, and I was so excited. To me, it was a great chance to prove that I deserved to be in the circle. I wanted to be the one with the ball in my hand when the game was on the line. The stands were packed. My family was there. Both teams were nationally ranked—we were No. 2 in the country, and the Sun Devils were No. 4. It was a great atmosphere.

But in the fourth inning, two players got on base against me. I made a mistake with a pitch, and the girl at the plate hit a three-run homer. While our team rallied in the seventh inning, we could only score once.

We lost the game 3–1. We lost to the rival Sun Devils. I had let down my team. Let down my school. Let down the Wildcat fans.

Usually after a loss I can hold myself together. I take pride in being composed, win or lose. But after that game I was completely devastated. I walked over to my parents after the game and buried my head in my dad's chest, fighting back the tears.

I managed to blurt out, "Dad, I never want to lose again."

I was wrecked. It hurt so much. It stung.

Believe me, I never thought something good could come out of a loss, particularly not a loss to ASU. But something did. That burning desire to never lose again fueled me every time I took the mound from then on. It wasn't that I had accepted losing before. But now my competitiveness kicked into overdrive. I was so angry and so determined. I wanted to make my words to my dad a reality.

I didn't lose for the rest of that season. And I didn't lose the next season, compiling a perfect 32–0 record while helping my team win the national championship at the College World Series. By the time I lost another game—midway through my senior year—I had put together a 60-game winning streak to set an NCAA record.

If you had told me in Tempe—when I was so downcast and heartbroken and crying in my father's arms like a little girl—that moment was going to produce something wonderful, I would have scoffed at you. No way.

But something changed in me that night. I learned something about myself. I learned to dig deeper. To find a toughness I didn't know I had. To welcome the challenge in front of me. To take my game to the next level.

It might also be the moment that I really learned that—to quote the great Billie Jean King—pressure is a privilege.

EMBRACE THE HEAT

Like so many girls, I felt a lot of pressure growing up. And along the way I learned that there are different kinds of pressure.

There's the bad kind that overwhelms you and presses down on you, and you feel you can't control it. Then there's the good pressure, the kind that is the result of people expecting a lot out of you—believing in you. Pressure because you've been given something important and meaningful to do—because you have a purpose.

Being a pitcher taught me to embrace that good kind of pressure. I liked having the ball in my hands. I liked being in control of something. I enjoyed being involved in every play of the game when we were on the field. I knew it was a lot of responsibility. My dad always reminded me that, as the pitcher, I was the one whose name would be listed in the paper with either a W or an L next to it. I knew my teammates were counting on me. I welcomed that position.

Rather than chafe against that pressure, I tried to embrace it. I wanted to prove I was worthy of it. I knew that having that kind of pressure meant great responsibility and potentially great rewards.

When I got to the University of Arizona, I really started to understand the importance of welcoming pressure. Being the top recruit in a high-profile program was very intense at such a great sports school.

I loved being at Arizona and being part of the college sports scene. I loved living in an apartment with my softball teammates. I loved getting all my red and blue Wildcats gear and being part of something so much bigger than myself. A Wildcat. One of many.

I loved hanging out at the McKale center and meeting so many of the athletes on campus. What a thrill it was to find out how many of them were tall. I finally felt comfortable enough to wear heels! The athletic department felt like family; it made an enormous campus seem so much smaller. I always encourage girls to try to find something at school that they can be part of to help make the experience more personal.

It wasn't always easy being on my own. Sure a part of me was excited about being independent and in control of my own schedule. But I was homesick and called my parents almost every day. And it was difficult without my dad/pitching coach helping me, pushing me, and not letting me slack.

My new freedom came with a price. My results weren't there. And I wasn't really sure why—I thought I was working so hard, but it was difficult for me to tell. College is a different experience, and no one

"Life's challenges are not supposed to paralyze you. They're supposed to help you discover who you are."
—Bernice Johnson Reagon, Amercian singer and composer

I feel the pressure to be a good role model every time I sign an autograph.
(AP Images)

was looking over me. The coaches expect you to be responsible. For example, they didn't use a radar gun on me, so I was unsure of my speed while I was pitching. I was learning about strength training and lifting weights, which was a whole new experience. I was learning to compete at a completely different level, a level where the players were all great and they could handle my pitches. I was learning how to handle the schedule of being a student/athlete.

I knew I was the No. 2 pitcher on our team even though it was never stated or said. And while I would never show my teammates or coaches that I didn't like it, on the inside it ate me up. I hadn't been the No. 2 pitcher since I was in grade school. Eventually, I settled into that role and accepted it my freshman year. I was the youngest on the team. I hadn't earned anything yet.

But I wasn't happy or satisfied with the way things were going on the softball field. I felt like I wasn't doing as well as I should. Because I was the No. 2 pitcher, when we had doubleheaders I would play first base in the first game and pitch the second game. Because I knew I was going to pitch, I was always concerned about saving my legs. I never wanted to eat in between games because I didn't like eating right before I pitched. So I was always hungry.

I was out of my comfort zone and focusing on the negatives, like my tired legs. It was a huge lesson. I needed to learn to bring it, to be ready to go, to give my coach and teammates whatever they needed and not focus on the other stuff.

I was able to contribute to the team by playing first base. I have always taken pride in being a complete player. Since I wasn't completely satisfied with my pitching, playing first eased the sting a little.

After I came home for the summer, I rededicated myself. I was determined I was going to do better. I wasn't going to just settle for being No. 2. I'd had a year to adjust to college life, and I knew what to expect. College sports were no longer an unknown. I came back for my sophomore year with a new fire. And it paid off.

Until that night against ASU.

That awful loss made me so angry. It made me realize that if I was going to be the pitcher I knew I could be, I was going to have to battle. I was going to have to earn the confidence of my teammates, to prove that they could trust me when the game was on the line. I was determined to show that I was more than just a big-name recruit out of high school. I vowed to be known as something more than that pitcher who had let Arizona State win for the first time in 39 games. I planned to turn all my frustration into determination through hard work.

I was going to take all that pressure and do something good with it.

SNAKE BLOOD AND BUG BITES

At the same time I was navigating college, I was learning to deal with another form of pressure—being on the Junior U.S. national team, representing USA Softball and my country.

My first USA National team experience had been when I was 16 and invited to tryouts at the Olympic Festival. I was so nervous, and I felt so young. I knew how much it meant to wear that USA jersey. I was so honored, and I wanted to make sure I wore it with respect for the people who had worn it before me.

The next time I was invited to try out, I was a freshman in college. I tried out and made the Junior National team. It was very nerve-wracking. At the Olympic Training Center in San Diego, they posted the names of the girls who had made the team on the facility door. Only about 17 of the almost 50 players who had tried out made it. Girls were standing in front of the door, crying and angry. When I saw my name, I felt awe and relief.

"Never fear shadows. They simply mean there's a light shining somewhere nearby."
—Ruth Renkel, inspirational speaker

My Favorite Player

Growing up, I wanted to be like Orel Hershiser. I loved the way he approached pitching, and I liked reading anything he wrote or hearing anything he said abut baseball.

Here are some excerpts from his book, *Out of the Blue*:

Baseball is a game, but there's nothing fun or funny about a fastball or a line drive screaming off the bat. That's why I narrow the game to priority No. 1: *the pitch*.

And what goes into that pitch? I break the task into four major areas: Attitude, Mechanics, Strategy, Regimen.

These all overlap, of course. The right attitude with wrong mechanics results in failure. The right attitude and the right mechanics with the wrong strategy hunts the same result. Your attitude, your belief in yourself, your ability, and your mechanics, these allow you more strategy options.

If every pitch is thrown with the right mechanics and is rooted in sound strategy, the results will take care of themselves.

I never try to show up an umpire. I don't see any future in it. That's all part of pitching strategy, too. They have a job to do, and it doesn't do me any good to try to make them look bad, even if they do make a mistake. I make mistakes, too, but I wouldn't want an umpire glaring at me because of it.

Once my catcher and I determine the pitch, that's all there is. There's nobody standing there, I don't think about the next game, the next inning, the next hitter, the next play. There's only the next pitch. It's the only job I have.

A prepared pitcher is more likely to win, than a lucky one...

Pitching is an art. Without a wide selection of pitches thrown properly for maximum effect, the artist is limited. One of the major elements in pitching strategy, as you will see, is surprise. If you have only two or three pitches and they always look the same, no hitter will be surprised. That's how dependent strategy is on mechanics. You can have mechanics with no strategy, but without mechanics, there is no strategy.

Proper mechanics allow a pitcher to align his body in such a way that all his power and energy and speed and strength [are] concentrated in making his arm the perfect lever for delivering the ball to the plate.

The Junior World Championships were in Taipei, Taiwan. It was my first time out of the country, other than a trip across the California border to Tijuana. What an eye-opening experience. I was so naïve about the rest of the world. We didn't have the comfortable towels or bedding I was accustomed to. One of my teammates got such a bad bug bite that her eye was swollen shut when she woke up in the morning, and another woke up with a swollen hand. The food was stuff I had never even seen—one of my teammates drank snake's blood, and during a visit to the night market we saw worms and eyeballs, animal feet and brains. It was my first experience in learning to survive for many days on peanut butter and jelly.

It was also the first time that I learned about the aura of USA Softball, the dominance of our squad, and how the other countries viewed us. When we walked on the field, you could hear people say, "Ooooh, USA." I felt so proud representing my country.

And for the first time I realized how incredibly fortunate I was. We had such great uniforms and equipment, and some teams didn't have anything nearly as nice as ours. We had brought extra equipment and gear to give away, and you could see how much it meant to other teams, how they looked at us as some kind of superstars. The other players would even ask us for our autographs after the game. They would take pictures with us and want our pins. It felt odd that they knew so much about us and we didn't know much about them.

But we were learning. In that tournament, we lost to Japan in the gold medal game—a foreshadowing of the parity that would be coming and would impact the rest of my career. Yukiko Ueno pitched in that game, and I remember thinking, *Wow, she's good*. We lost the game on two infield ground balls to shortstop; Japan had so much speed. It really struck me that they didn't play the same style that we did, not at all.

Our loss was a big deal because USA Softball didn't lose very often, if ever. That experience really made me realize the pressure that comes with representing the United States.

After that, I earned a spot on the National team. I felt like I had made it to the *real* National team, with the superstars I had grown up idolizing. I never felt secure with my spot on the National team—at every tryout I worried that I wouldn't make it and that someone else was going to take my spot. There was so much talent at every tryout, it really kept everyone on edge.

Traveling the world and representing USA Softball and my country was such an honor. We played in places like Venezuela, Brazil, the Dominican Republic, Canada, and Japan. Sometimes we had to have armed guards with us because of turmoil in the country we were visiting. Sometimes we were booed by the crowd. At times, especially after September 11, 2001, we felt like targets. We knew we always had the metaphorical target on our back—every team wanted to beat USA Softball.

It was always an adventure seeing how other cultures lived. And despite concerns about security, each experience was uplifting. I was always so moved at seeing how sports can bring together people of all different types and backgrounds. Despite the language barriers and cultural differences, we were a community on the softball field.

And everywhere we went, we felt the pride and pressure of representing the United States of America and we knew how blessed we were.

DIAMONDBACKS AND RED CARPETS

Things started to get crazy for me.

At Arizona, my junior year in 2001, we had a fantastic season and won a national championship. That was so thrilling. When I got to Arizona, I thought I might win multiple national championships—after all, the program already had won five. But I quickly learned that just having Arizona across your chest was no guarantee of anything. A championship took so much hard work and sacrifice.

> *"Don't wait until everything is just right. It will never be perfect. There will always be challenges, obstacles, and less-than-perfect conditions. So what? Get started now. With each step you take you will grow stronger and stronger, more and more skilled, more and more self-confident, and more and more successful."*
> —Mark Victor Hansen, motivational speaker

Our team was getting a lot of recognition. In my freshman year, only one of our games had been televised. By my senior year, every single one of our games was on television.

My world was spinning so fast. I was crafting a 60-game undefeated streak into my senior year. I had been named the Honda Player of the Year for softball as a junior, and I won the award again my senior year. I had also been named the College World Series MVP. The buildup for the 2004 Olympics was happening. Oh, and on top of it all, I was in the midst of falling in love with my future husband.

I call this time in my life "the explosion." One minute I was a kid trying to prove that I could be my team's top pitcher and get a college education. The next minute—or so it seemed—I was riding a tidal wave of publicity and opportunity. And, of course, more pressure.

That time period is all such a huge blur. Things kept happening that didn't seem quite real. For example, the Arizona Diamondbacks had just won the World Series in 2001. The next season, for the cover of their Diamondback fan magazine, they did a big cover story on "Arizona's Best Pitcher." On the cover? Randy Johnson, Curt Schilling—and me. During the photo shoot I kept thinking, *How in the world did I get here?*

In Tucson, our team had a huge fan base and were recognized everywhere we went. We were asked to be the Grand Marshals in

Life started to get crazy for me, but Casey supported me every step of the way.
(AP Images)

a local Tucson parade, along with the Diamondbacks—and the major league ballplayers all knew who we were. After I completed my eligibility but was still in school, I started getting opportunities for well-paying jobs, working at softball clinics. I was receiving so many requests for appearances and interviews and I was dealing with contracts and executives; pretty soon I realized I needed an agent to handle everything.

But even with guidance, I didn't know how to handle the onslaught. I didn't know when to say no and when to say yes. So I kept saying yes. I had so many obligations that on my few days off I was running around at a frantic pace from one commitment to the next.

*   *   *   *

This was a new kind of pressure for me. It didn't have anything to do with being on the mound or trying to strike out a batter. It didn't have to do with competition. It was unfamiliar.

As with softball, I felt an obligation and that I was responsible for something. I knew that every time I did an interview or was on a TV show that it was great publicity for our sport and women's sports overall. I felt a huge responsibility to USA Softball and wanted to make sure that everyone knew about our fabulous team. Suddenly, much to my surprise, I had a platform to tell the world about our sport and our awesome athletes. I didn't want to waste it.

I knew that I was getting the kind of mainstream attention that the great players who played just a few years earlier had never received. I'll never forget how excited Lisa Fernandez—the best player in our game, who had been on the National team since 1991 and is nine years older than I am—was about all the opportunities I had. She wasn't bitter that she hadn't had the same kinds of opportunities. She was just psyched that it was happening. She wanted to know all about the appearances and who I had met. Her enthusiasm and encouragement (along with that of my other teammates) made it more fun for me.

But at times it seemed like too much for me to handle. For one thing, I wasn't comfortable doing interviews. At first, after every one, I would beat myself up—I felt like I had sounded so dumb and naïve. I just didn't have much confidence. I was so young and raw and hadn't had any kind of media training.

For another thing, I had an obligation to be in shape for the national team. I know that Coach Candrea—who by that time had been named the head coach of the U.S. National team—was concerned that I was spreading myself too thin. I had finished my college eligibility, so it was really up to me to stay in shape. For years, my dad had guided me, then college provided the structure. But now I was on my own—in charge of my own body and routines. If I didn't do the work, I wasn't going to make the Olympic team.

So I spent a lot of time second-guessing myself. Should I fly to New York to do an appearance on David Letterman? Or head to L.A. for a red carpet awards show? Or should I stay home and train and rest? Of course, I usually chose to do the appearance, get on a plane, and promise myself I would extra hard when I got back. And I would try to find a way to workout when I was on the road. Several times I pitched in New York's Central Park. I searched out batting cages. I went to alleyways behind hotels. I sought out high school and collegiate catchers to help me with my workouts from all over the U.S.

And—of course—in between those appearances, I would try to squeeze in a quick visit with Casey.

Sometimes I have wondered how much better a pitcher and player I would have been if I had managed to have a more consistent routine. I believe that consistency is a big part of preparation and performance. Coach Candrea scheduled our days off so we would have time to regroup and relax. That's how most of my teammates used the days off, but not me.

To be honest, I wasn't always doing what I knew might be best for my athletic performance. It was a battle between training and doing what I thought was good for my sport's visibility. I felt I had a fleeting

Working for This Week in Baseball *was an incredible opportunity.*

opportunity to promote my sport and I believed—especially in the lead up to the Athens Olympics—that was one of my jobs. Who knew when this window of exposure might shut?

Even after so many years playing sports, I was still trying to figure it out.

I was aware that I was getting a chance to do things that few—if any—women had done before. Major League Baseball's weekly show

This Week in Baseball asked me to join their show. Every week, I had a segment called "Pinch, Hit, and Run with Jennie Finch." I had the opportunity to meet some of the greatest players in baseball, such as Barry Bonds, Roger Clemens, Jimmy Rollins, Randy Johnson, and Alex Rodriguez. I got the chance to pick the brains of these amazing athletes and talk, athlete-to-athlete, about preparation, strategy, and fundamentals. Sure, it was a job, but it was also a once-in-a-lifetime opportunity.

The *This Week in Baseball* people were fabulous—they took a naïve girl with a communications major from Arizona and helped me look decent on television. Thanks to the fantastic crew and all the help they gave me—and of course preparation and practice—I don't think I embarrassed myself too badly. They made me look like a rock star, and my mistakes were left in the editing room.

It was through *This Week in Baseball* that I found myself pitching to Paul Lo Duca at Dodger Stadium. The team I rooted for my entire life—including Tommy Lasorda, who had managed the team I worshipped, and legendary announcer Vin Scully—looked on while I pitched. They handed me my own Dodger uniform: Finch, No. 27. Talk about a dream come true!

I had to pinch myself when I was on the mound at Dodger Stadium, the very place I had daydreamed about as a little girl.

I struck out Lo Duca that day. In fact, during three seasons on *This Week in Baseball*, I struck out more than 35 hitters that I faced, including guys like Mike Piazza and Albert Pujols. It made me proud to see big leaguers walking away from the plate, shaking their heads in amazement. Some didn't even want to face me because they knew they'd get a hard time from their teammates.

Then I got to Angel Stadium and was facing a feared Angels hitter named Scott Spiezio. I got two strikes against him on rise balls—something MLB players aren't used to. I went to strike out Scott with my change-up—like I usually did—and he smashed the ball to second base. He was the first major league player to make

> *"Success is not the result of spontaneous combustion.*
> *You must set yourself on fire."*
> —Fred Shero, hockey coach

contact off me! I was bummed out about that. My perfect record was gone.

Scott was taking an enthusiastic victory lap, and his team was going wild like they'd just won the World Series. After his trot and celebration, he called over to me.

"Hey Finch, you need to mix it up!"

I didn't understand what he meant.

"Excuse me?" I asked.

"There's a scouting report on you up here," Scott said. "I knew the third pitch was going to be a change-up."

That actually took the sting out of losing my streak against the guys. How cool was it to find out there was a scouting report on me in the big leagues?

I learned that day that guys actually like to gossip and talk smack as much as the girls do. And I also learned this: girls, if you ever want to strike out a guy, stick to the rise ball. They're not used to it.

THE ONGOING PROCESS

Pressure doesn't really go away in life. It's not like you reach a point and you think, "Okay. I'm done. I've accomplished everything."

I feel daily pressure to improve, learn, and be a better person. I feel pressure every time I make an appearance or host a camp for 400 girls from 16 different states. I feel it every time I sign an autograph. My hope is to connect, inspire, motivate, listen—to be worthy of someone's interest and attention. Believe me, it is an absolute privilege to have that kind of pressure.

Despite my vow that night in Tempe, I did—of course—lose again, unfortunately. Losing is part of sports. A part of the process.

We aren't perfect. My teammate Laura Berg, who was the only four-time softball Olympian, was always hard on herself when she was growing up. But her coach used to tell her, "When you can walk on water, come talk to me. Until then, get over it." She is one of my favorite and most amazing teammates. She always gave 110% no matter what.

My personal winning streak in college had kind of taken on a life of its own. I hadn't set out to break any kind of record. I just wanted to give my team the best chance to win a national championship. And I certainly didn't want my winning streak to end at the College World Series.

It didn't. Coach Candrea had me pitch the championship game against UCLA, and we won 1–0. It was the greatest feeling ever, especially knowing that our eight seniors would be finally leaving with a national championship. They didn't become the first Arizona softball class to never win a championship.

The winning streak went into the next year, my senior year. The national media realized I was closing in on an NCAA record, and I started getting a lot of attention. I felt a ton of pressure because I was one of only two seniors on that year's team—along with eight freshmen—and we wanted to repeat as national champions. To me, it was all about the team. I didn't really want the focus to be on me.

I matched and then broke the existing record of 50 straight wins. Midway through Pac-10 competition of my senior year, we were playing top-ranked UCLA at home. I came in to relieve in the second inning with the score tied. An Olympic gold medalist and All-American named Stacey Nuveman hit a home run off me in the fourth inning and another one—which blasted off the scoreboard with the loudest bang I'd ever heard—in the seventh. That last one won the game for UCLA. We had to watch them celebrate on our home field.

The streak was over, but I didn't really care about the streak, I cared about the loss. I was just so mad that we had lost to UCLA and at home. The streak wasn't the important thing. Our team's success was what counted. We made it back to the NCAA championship game that year but ended up losing to California.

And I took the loss in that game, my last collegiate game.

When it was over, I sat in the dugout at Hall of Fame Stadium in Oklahoma City, crying and heartbroken. I stared out at the field, realizing that my collegiate career was finished and that I was done competing for my beloved Wildcats.

I was the last one still in the dugout. Coach Candrea came over and asked me if I was ready to leave.

I stood up and came out of the dugout. And then I saw a line of people stretching from our dugout all the way down the left-field line and around the outfield fence.

"What is this?" I asked Coach.

"They want your autograph," he said.

I couldn't believe it. Why did they want my autograph? Hadn't I just lost?

But I was honored to sign for them. I was in awe—people were holding up signs and saying thank you to me. I signed and I signed and I signed. While I was still heartbroken over the loss, the experience made me realize that what had just happened was so much bigger than one loss, even bigger than one national championship.

It was about the sport and opportunity. It was about the chance to touch others and to inspire dreams.

It was a privilege.

Jennie's Tips on Stepping Up to a Challenge

1. Prepare. You might only get one chance, one opportunity. So be ready when it comes along!

2. Focus on the positives. Don't dwell on what's not working—like tired legs. Think about your strengths!

3. Enjoy the moment. Too often the big moments in life go by in a blur. I love it when I see an athlete looking up at the stands, soaking it all in. Take a second to appreciate where you are.

4. Accept help. Don't be afraid to ask your coaches, family, and friends for advice and guidance.

5. Trust it and execute it. Trust your preparation and practice. And once you're in the moment, execute.

Chapter 13

Being a Role Model:
Accepting the
Big Responsibility

When I was in my early twenties, my world was changing so fast it made my head spin. I was getting offers to do all sorts of things: represent companies, appear on television shows, and walk the red carpet at awards shows.

It was overwhelming and exciting and, to be honest, sometimes it was hard to keep my feet on the ground. But there were a couple of opportunities that were easy to turn down. When men's magazines asked me to pose for them.

They were extremely lucrative offers—more money than I could have dreamed of just to take some pictures. It was tempting, but I knew there was no way I could do those photo shoots.

I'm careful about what projects I give the thumbs-up to! (AP Images)

Even though I knew it didn't feel right, it took my brother, Landon, to really make the point to me about why I didn't want to do those kinds of things.

"Jennie, what if some little girl sees that magazine in a store and because you're her favorite player she wants her parents to buy it for her?" Landon said. "How are you going to feel if the parents can't buy it because it's inappropriate?"

I knew exactly how I would feel. I would be heartbroken.

But I tried to rationalize, arguing that the article I was in would be fine. Landon, however, pointed out that the other articles wouldn't be suitable, that parents wouldn't be comfortable with their daughter having such a magazine. He was right, of course.

Sure, doing those photo shoots could have earned me money. But I needed to step outside myself and see how it would affect others. I would have lost my self-respect and the respect of many young girls and their families. I had so much more to lose than to gain.

Being a role model is something I take very seriously. It's a big responsibility, but knowing that girls look up to me makes many of my career and life decisions that much easier.

THE GOLDEN RULE

When I was in middle school, I went to the college near my house to watch a collegiate softball game. I waited and waited and waited after the game to get the autograph of one of my favorite players. I was so excited and nervous. I admired her so much. I wanted to be just like her.

And when she came off the field, she just walked right past me without a glance. I was heartbroken. As it turns out, I found out I didn't want to be just like one of my heroes. I wanted to be nicer.

I vowed right then that if I was ever so lucky that a young girl—or anyone—actually wanted my autograph, I would never blow her off. I pledged to try to treat people the way I would want to be treated.

> *"Life is 10 percent what happens to us and 90 percent how we react to it."*
> —Dennis P. Kimbro, motivational speaker

I've tried very hard to live by that lesson. At times my friends or coaches or husband get a little irritated with me because I will stay behind and sign and sign and sign until the last girl gets the autograph she was hoping for. Maybe it means I'll be late to dinner or that I'll be the last one out the building. I try to live by the Golden Rule—treat others the way you would like to be treated.

Everyone can make an impact just by taking an extra moment, by making one small gesture.

That memory of my own hurt feelings when I was denied an autograph sticks with me even until today. I can be brought right back to that moment of feeling so small and insignificant and that all my respect and adulation was misdirected.

I want every girl I meet to know how much I appreciate her support—and to know that one day, not that long ago, I was just like her.

HONORING THE GAME

A big part of being a role model, I believe, is honoring the people who came before me and the spirit of their accomplishments. I feel it is my obligation to pay tribute to those who paved the way and try to uphold their legacy and continue the momentum they started.

I've been so blessed to be able to get to know some of the trailblazers who changed the role of women in sports—and in doing so helped change the world. Women like tennis legend Billie Jean King and Olympic swimmer Donna de Varona, who were both involved in founding the Women's Sports Foundation. They have become some of my personal role models, and when I think about being a role model for others, I only hope I can be a little like those great pioneers.

To be honest, I didn't know too much about the history of girls and sports until after I had already achieved many of my athletic dreams. I had heard of Title IX, the federal law that prevents gender discrimination in institutions that receive federal funding. And I knew that times were changing. I had so much more opportunity than not only my grandmother or my mother but even girls who were just a few years older than me.

All those opportunities I had to do interviews and endorse products and appear on television? My teammates Lisa Fernandez and Dot Richardson—legends of our game, the faces of our sport—never had the chance to step into the cultural mainstream. They had their names on bats and were recognized inside the softball world. Every time I would tell Lisa about some new thing that came along—David Letterman or ESPN—she would be so pumped up. The world had totally changed in just a few years, and I was able to take advantage of those changes.

I happily welcomed this new opportunity, but I didn't spend a lot of time dwelling on how it had been achieved. I don't think I appreciated the struggles that had come before me.

And the little that I did know about Title IX was generally negative. When I heard it mentioned, it was usually in the context of how the law was taking opportunity away from boys and not how much it had done to help girls. Growing up, I heard a lot of comments about how it was mostly boys who *really* cared about sports and that Title IX was hurting them. Women who supported Title IX were almost always portrayed as being radical feminists.

"Each person must live their life as a model for others."
—Rosa Parks, civil rights pioneer

On the *Sports Illustrated* Swimsuit Issue

There was one invitation that came my way that I accepted even though some people in my family thought I shouldn't.

I agreed to pose for the *Sports Illustrated* Swimsuit Issue.

It was an exciting opportunity. We went to the Bahamas for the photo shoot. Along with a few other 2004 Olympians, I was asked to wear gold bathing suits—gold representing the Olympic medal I had won in Athens.

I thought it would be cool to be in *Sports Illustrated*—I used to scour *SI for Kids* when I was young, looking for something about girls in sports. I rarely found it back then. But I thought it would be fine to do a photo shoot for a sports magazine.

Looking back, I laugh at how naïve I was. For one thing, I'd never really looked at the swimsuit issue. And for another thing, I had no idea what a big deal it was and that it is considered a pinnacle in the modeling business—a business I didn't know much about.

I was excited that they asked me, an athlete who wears a size 8, to be in the magazine rather than just super models. I'm proud of my body and proud of my muscles. I don't look like a model—I might be tall, but I'm definitely not a size zero. So I was excited to show that a woman's body doesn't have to fit one standard. We can be strong, broad-shouldered, and well-muscled. A size 8 can be beautiful, too.

I wish I had worked out a little more leading up to the trip. I was in my post-Olympic relaxation mode. I'm not going to lie—I even ate lobster mac and cheese the night before the shoot at the hotel.

I had no idea what I was getting myself into. I have to admit I'm fairly uncomfortable in a bathing suit lying around the pool, let alone in front of a bunch of cameras.

The photographer could tell how clueless I was about posing. He tried to help me out. He even had to pose for me to provide an example, and he was better than me! And I was uncomfortable with all the people watching the photo shoot.

My favorite part was when I was able to slip on the comfy white terry cloth towel and sit on the beach! To be honest, I would have loved some more mac and cheese, too.

I also learned that once you do something like that, you better be happy with it because you can never get away from it. If you do a Google search of me, you're going to immediately see pictures of me in that gold bathing suit in the Bahamas. When I do autograph sessions, invariably some fan will bring the Swimsuit Issue for me to sign, which gives me a stomachache. I always want to ask, "Really? Still?"

It's a good lesson, though one I try to share with girls. Once you've taken pictures or video, they'll always be out there. The choices you make today can affect you later on.

I hear so much about girls losing a scholarship or getting in big trouble with a coach or a school because of pictures they've posted on Facebook or sent on their phone. Some coaches have to monitor Facebook to make sure their athletes and recruits are behaving appropriately. A small choice you make now can turn into a big ordeal down the road. Once you do something, those photos are going to live with you forever.

So choose wisely!

After I won an Olympic gold medal in Athens, I was asked by the Women's Sports Foundation to join a group of leaders and athletes going to Capitol Hill to raise awareness and support for Title IX. At the time, some lawmakers wanted to weaken the law. The Women's Sports Foundation wanted to make its case to keep the law strong by bringing along both legendary activists and younger athletes who represented the new generation in women's sports.

I'll admit I was a little nervous about going. Did I want to be branded as an activist? Or a radical?

But by taking part in the trip to Washington D.C. I learned so much—about the history of women's sports and therefore my own history. I heard Billie Jean and Donna speak about their struggles. I learned how far we had come in just a very short time. And I heard the stark reality of how far we still had to go.

I realized, really for the first time, that I was one of the direct beneficiaries of all the hard work that had come before me. I understood why the women who were pioneers had been radical—they didn't have any choice. They were simply trying to get a toehold in a completely male-dominated world. If they hadn't pushed, they would have been ignored.

And without them the rest of us wouldn't be here—not the fabulous Williams sisters in tennis or the soccer World Cup champions or the WNBA or the great women's collegiate programs all around the nation. We all owe the pioneers a tremendous debt. Without those women who came before me, there would be no Jennie Finch, softball pitcher. I would never have had the chance.

Because of those tireless women, I had so much opportunity. And I also had the option to not be radical or pushy. I could just play without having to fight every inch of the way. I hadn't realized how lucky I was until that week in Washington D.C.

It was very eye-opening to be immersed in the political world. We were instantly put on the defensive and were portrayed as if we were asking for things that weren't our right. The implication was that we didn't really deserve to have the same opportunities as men. I could see why women had to be radical to effect change.

That experience has made me feel strongly that women need to band together and share information with each other. We need to help each other, whether it comes to information about our own history, navigating the business world, or sharing what kind of financial gains are available to us. Male athletes do that easily. Women, too often, seem reluctant to share. But by not sharing information, we make ourselves weaker. We need to bond together and encourage each other.

I came away from Capitol Hill that week with a strong desire to be more vocal in my own support of women's sports. I was inspired to study and learn my own history. I felt I had a duty. I owed it to those before me and to those who will come after. I am of the firm belief that girls should learn about the past and not take their opportunities for granted.

You need to know that things can be taken away at any minute.

Sadly, I learned that lesson around the same time and in the most painful way imaginable. The International Olympic Committee decided to drop softball from the Olympics a year after we won the gold medal in Athens.

We were all shocked.

The decision was made by an organization—the IOC—whose membership is overwhelmingly composed of older men. Our sport was linked to a men's sport—baseball—that was considered superfluous to the Olympic movement. The IOC was not a fan of baseball because the best players didn't play, the game had been tarnished by doping issues, and the Olympics weren't vital to baseball. Baseball has the World Series.

But none of those issues applied to us. Our best players did participate. We didn't have doping issues. And softball only had the Olympics. That was our World Series.

I love the sport of baseball, and I'm married to a baseball player, but I knew that our sport deserved to stand on its own. We are our own

> *"Character is doing the right thing*
> *when nobody's looking."*
> —J.C. Watts, football player

entity and have our own national governing body. Why were we being judged by the standards of a men's sport?

I was devastated and dumbfounded. Our sport was wildly successful. Our ratings and popularity had never been bigger. We had just been named America's "Real Dream Team" by *Sports Illustrated*.

Every year, things had been moving forward for softball and getting better. More opportunity was created and progress was constant. But that all vanished in one vote. All the dreams of so many girls were snuffed out in an instant.

As a role model who wanted to leave the game in better shape than when I found it, I was crushed.

STAYING TRUE TO YOURSELF

The men's magazines weren't the only lucrative offers I've turned down. I've rejected reality shows and liquor commercials. I don't want to do things that might make a girl ask, "Why is Jennie Finch doing that?"

My parents and my faith always taught me right from wrong. So I try to operate on my gut instincts and my heart.

During the time I call "the explosion," I had so many opportunities and felt like I was being pulled in so many directions that it was hard to stay grounded. I met a lot of famous people. I had some odd interactions that illustrated the ways in which famous people are catered to by others and how many of them expect to receive preferential treatment. I saw up close that reaching the pinnacle of success is no guarantee of happiness. I saw how easy it would be for a young, naïve person to get caught up in the overwhelming culture of celebrity. At times, I found myself getting caught up in "it." It's so easy to do when surrounded by "worldly" things.

That happens to young people a lot—they get a little taste of fame and money and suddenly their whole world spins out of control. I think too much of our culture sends the message that wealth and celebrity

I couldn't have had my career without the hard work of all the women who came before me. (AP Images)

> *"Time has a wonderful way of showing us what really matters."*
> —Margaret Peters, educator

are all that's truly important. I feel so sad when I see beautiful young actresses who have become society's punch lines because they lost control of their lives.

I believe it's really important to stay true to yourself and who you are.

My family provided me with a foundation and helped me stay grounded, even when my world began to change. I've always tried to honor that foundation. I don't ever want to be in a position that would embarrass my family, my friends, or my fans.

THE NEXT GENERATION

What's the best part of my softball career?

It's getting to interact with young girls, hearing their dreams and their goals, and getting the opportunity to encourage them to believe in themselves and reach for the stars. When parents tell me that I'm a role model for their daughter, it warms my heart.

The thing about an athletic career is that it all goes by so fast. You can get caught up in the daily grind, in worrying about yourself, your fitness, and the competition. Sometimes I have to remind myself to step back and look at the big picture. When I look out on all those eager faces at one of my camps, I'm so psyched. Those moments help me appreciate that our sport is so much more than a game.

I love meeting girls and hearing their stories. There's a girl named Stevie from Chino Hills in California who had a serious knee injury. When she was on the road to recovery, she came to one of my camps. She told me that my motto "Dream and Believe" helped get her through her toughest days of the pain and rehabilitation. I was so honored. She is holding on to her dream of playing in college. And I know she's going to do it.

Stevie is the kind of girl who's going to make things happen. She's a fighter. She has a positive outlook, and I don't think she'll take no for an answer. I can tell she's going to be a great role model. Actually, she already is—I noticed the other girls watching her on the field and listening closely when she had something to say. You don't need to be older or more experienced to be a strong role model. It's all in your attitude and leadership. Someone is always watching you—a younger sibling or friends at school.

Girls like Stevie are going to make a difference. I feel so optimistic that the sport is in good hands!

Jennie's Tips on Being a Role Model

1. Embrace it. You might not know it, but you are a role model to someone in your life. It might be a little sister, a teammate, or a child you babysit. It might be someone down the street that you barely know. But understand—you have made an impression on someone in your life. Honor it!

2. Always conduct yourself like someone's watching. Don't do anything that would make you embarrassed if it was caught on film—or posted on Facebook. Like the quote from J.C. Watts says, "Character is doing the right thing when nobody's looking."

3. Think about your actions from the point of view of others. If this was my friend, would I be proud of her? If that was my daughter, would I feel good about her behavior? It's the simple Golden Rule: treat others as you would like to be treated yourself.

4. Honor the past. Think about the women who came before you, who didn't have the same kind of opportunities for education or athletics or careers. Represent them in what you do and respect their legacy.

5. Look at the big picture. Try to look outside of yourself, and take the opportunity to do something for others.

Chapter 14

Winning and Losing

In 1996, the world seemed like a place of limitless opportunity.

I was 15, and my world revolved around softball. And for the first time, softball was going to be in the Summer Olympics. The greatest players in my game were on sports' biggest stage. I was so excited.

Even better, the Olympic team was coming to my area. A few weeks before the Atlanta Olympics, I went to watch the Olympians at Mayfair Park in Lakewood, California, not far from my house.

I still get chills thinking about that night. My parents and I got there about four hours before game time. Our seats were right by the dugout—close enough to see and hear and soak in everything those players did. They seemed like superheroes to me, floating around on the field in their red, white, and blue uniforms.

That night, I could see my dreams and goals right there in front of me. I wanted to be just like them. I wanted to have "USA" written across my chest. I wanted to feel what it was like to bow my head and have a gold medal slipped around my neck.

I think we were the very last ones to leave the park that night. I waited in line for all the players' autographs after the game. I was so excited I could barely sleep when I got home. I couldn't wait to get to practice the next day and start turning my dreams into reality.

I was dreaming. I was believing. Big time.

GOLD MEDALS AND TEARS

Eight years later, I was standing on a medal podium in Athens, Greece.

Those eight years had sped by in an amazing rush of hard work, new experiences, practice, sweat, laughter, tears, frustration, innings, and joy.

My path from Olympic dreams to Olympic reality wasn't a clear, upward trajectory. There were plenty of bumps along the way. But I always tried to find the positive during the tough times. I think there are life lessons to be gained from your struggles if you allow yourself to grow and learn.

Very few experiences in life are either completely good or totally bad. Usually there's a mix of both that helps you keep things in perspective. I certainly found that out during my Olympic experiences.

In 2004, we were so prepared. We had trained so hard. We had such a fantastic team. The title "Dream Team" had been routinely given to the U.S. men's basketball team ever since NBA players started being allowed to play in the Olympics. But in Athens, our softball team was being called the "Real Dream Team" outscoring our opponents 54–1.

> *"The battles that count aren't the ones for gold medals. The struggles within yourself—the invisible, inevitable battles inside all of us—that's where it's at."*
> —Jesse Owens, Olympian

I was on the same team with some of my childhood heroes. A few years earlier, I had been asking them for their autographs. Now I was going to share the field with them.

That's why it stunned me when Coach Candrea, who became the Olympic coach prior to the Athens Games, told me that he wanted me to pitch our first game against Italy. When he told me, my eyes filled with tears. I felt so honored.

We arrived in Athens three weeks before the Games were to start. The Athletes' Village wasn't even complete. It was an ongoing joke. We'd wake up every morning and say, "Oh look, there are trees outside today." "Oh look, today we have a shower curtain." Things were changing every day in the preparation to get ready. But our team was there and already eager to start.

We didn't march in the Opening Ceremonies because we had a game the next day. I remember that when the veterans made that decision some of the younger girls were disappointed. Even though it was my first Olympics, I figured that the veterans knew what they were talking about. I had so much respect for them. I knew they were giving us the best chance to win. But it was very odd that night, sitting in the training room at the Athletes' Village, watching the beautiful Opening Ceremonies on TV. I was thinking, "Are we really here? It feels like we're still at home."

But we had to be up and ready early the next day. We had sacrificed so much for that moment. We didn't want to blow it.

We got to the stadium and realized that this was really it: the Olympics. The Olympic rings were out front. The stadium was a beautiful little ballpark right next to the sparkling blue Aegean Sea. The greatest athletes in the world were competing all around the city. It was spectacular.

I was beyond nervous. I had to keep telling myself to calm down. "Okay Jennie. This is still the same game."

When I stepped on the mound, my heart was beating out of my body. The atmosphere seemed surreal. But I was right. It was still the same game. After a pitch or two, I settled in and our team played great. We won that opener 7–0.

But I had to pull myself out in the third inning. On a pitch, I had torn an oblique muscle. After the game, we worked hard to rehabilitate the injury with ice and stim and medication before my next start. A sports psychologist worked with me on overcoming pain.

I made my next start against Canada and went the distance, pitching a one-hitter. I still don't know how I did it. I was in a lot of pain—no amount of sports psychology could make it go away. I felt it was definitely the Lord carrying me through every single pitch.

I was devastated. I couldn't believe the injury was really happening. I had had so few injuries in my entire career, and here—at the biggest moment of my life—I couldn't go.

Thank goodness we had three other pitchers who were the best in the world, including Lisa Fernandez. My childhood hero-now-teammate was on fire and pitched every game of the medal round. Eight years earlier I had been at Mayfair Park waiting for her autograph. Now Mayfair Park is named Lisa Fernandez Field. At the Athens Olympics she only added to her legendary status.

We didn't announce my injury to the media. There was no need to make it public: the team was on a roll, and I kept trying to convince myself I was going to get better. But I knew I couldn't be at my best. I was down in the bullpen trying to stay ready, but I really couldn't pitch.

Wrapped within all that difficulty and disappointment was a lesson in how to contribute. I wanted to do something, anything, for my team. I made sure the coaches knew I was available to pinch-run. I high-fived my teammates going on and coming off the field. I tried to

Standing on the podium in Athens to receive my gold medal was one of the highlights of my life.

stay completely positive—we had taken that long journey together, and even if I couldn't play, I wanted to make sure I did everything I could to ensure our success.

The night before the gold medal game against Australia, we packed our special gold-medal jackets into our bags. Everyone was nervous, excited. I was living out my dream.

We beat Australia 5–1 (the only run our pitching staff had allowed the entire tournament). I can't adequately describe my feelings of pride as I bowed my head to feel the gold medal draped around my neck and stood side-by-side with my great teammates. We watched our flag rise up on the tallest flagpole and heard the "Star-Spangled Banner" played for us.

I was thrilled.

That was the moment I'd been dreaming about, the moment I'd been waiting for forever. And then I saw Coach Candrea in the dugout with his son and daughter, sobbing in excitement but grieving also.

And I was completely humbled. God had chosen that moment to remind me that there is so much more to life than medals.

Our Olympic run had been wrapped in tragedy. A month before the Olympics, Coach's wife, Sue, had been waiting for a flight with our team when she had felt ill. She passed away two days later from a brain aneurysm. We were all shocked and devastated.

It put everything in perspective. We had all been traveling for half a year, away from our families. And we learned how quickly everything could be gone. It was a sobering lesson for a bunch of young women.

Sue's funeral was one of the saddest moments I've experienced. All through my time at Arizona, she had been like a team mom to us. I was a very close friend of their son, who was in my same class at U of A. I spent time at their house. Sue was often on tour with us. Coach had called her his best friend and foundation. They had been married 28 years. I—engaged to be married after the Olympics—couldn't begin to imagine the pain that he and their children, Mikel, and Michelle, were feeling.

Our team was dedicated to winning the gold medal. But Coach's tragedy made our determination even fiercer. He knew Sue would have wanted him to keep coaching, so he did. He told us that we were his strength, helping him get through that tough time. But he was our rock. He was so strong, it was amazing.

But at that Gold medal moment, as the anthem played and the reality of what we had accomplished flooded over all of us, Coach Candrea broke. He finally let out his grief.

I learned so much in that single moment. The highs in life are intertwined with the lows. Everything was put in perspective. Medals will tarnish. What's really important in life was made crystal clear. Our next breath is never guaranteed.

SILVER MEDAL AND DEVASTATION

Everything about the Beijing Olympics felt different from Athens.

We prepared for China with an enormous cloud over our heads. Only a year after our triumph in Athens, the International Olympic Committee voted to drop softball from Olympic competition.

The decision was like a knife to my heart. When the national team received the news, we were playing a tournament. Of course we were. We had all spent years of dedication and hard work, time away from our loved ones, playing the sport we loved. We felt we had served our sport well, helping it grow. We had great television ratings, a huge fan base, and young girls all over the world were picking up the sport. Our sport had never been bigger or more popular. Other countries finally had established their programs.

How could they do this to us and to millions of little girls?

The various explanations made no sense.

We heard that we were eliminated because we were tied to baseball. So why were we being punished? Unlike baseball, our best players *did* participate. We didn't have the equivalent of a World Series; for us the Olympics was our World Series.

We heard we were being eliminated because we were too dominating. The U.S. softball team won too much. But that didn't make any sense, either. Aren't the Olympics supposed to be about excellence? The IOC didn't toss out basketball when the American Dream Team was beating opponents by 40 points. After a few years, the NBA players on the Dream Team actually lost some games. The IOC might not have been able to see the growing parity in softball, but we

"You can learn a line from a win and a book from defeat."
—Paul Brown, football coach

could see it in every international tournament we played. We could see the gap narrowing.

We heard we were being eliminated because our sport was American-centric, without enough participation around the globe. But our sport is played in Asia, Australia, and South America. More that 140 countries play softball, and it is growing everywhere. The Olympics later added rugby, even though very few countries have women's rugby teams. The explanations just didn't make sense.

As young women we were shocked. The IOC—an organization dominated by older men—paid lip service to gender equity. Yet it had just cavalierly eliminated a popular team sport for women, a sport that required great athletic ability and was played by women of all different shapes and sizes. It was the kind of discrimination and narrow-mindedness that most of us had never faced.

All we'd known in our lives as athletes was progress. Women's sports opportunities were supposed to grow, not be taken away. But now we were going backward. It was so hard to fathom, and it still is. Unfortunately, it's reality.

Our focus became Beijing. We felt that the best thing we could do to defend our sport was put on a great show. Coach told us over and over that we needed to play the game the best it's ever been played. We needed to take advantage of the Olympic platform to showcase our sport.

But the buildup to Beijing felt so different. I know I was different because I had Ace. In 2008, I was hungry and eager to get back. But, as a mom, my feeling of team camaraderie wasn't quite as carefree. I had new responsibilities.

Lisa Fernandez had also started her own family. She had been out of international competition for a couple of years. She came back to try out for the team the winter before the Olympics. And shockingly, when the Olympic roster was named and the alternates were selected, Lisa was an alternate. That happened in March—very late in the process—and it caused big shock waves throughout our team that continued to reverberate for a long time.

On Olympic Ideals

I feel so honored to have participated in two Olympic Games. The Olympics are such an incredible tradition. There is no other gathering on our planet bringing together people from so many countries all in the name of peace and sport.

Behind all the pomp and circumstance are some incredibly meaningful ideals:

- **The Olympic Creed:** This is the guiding principle of the Games. "The most important thing in the Olympic Games is not to win but to take part, just as the most important thing in life is not the triumph but the struggle. The essential thing is not to have conquered but to have fought well."
- **The Olympic Motto:** This is meant to spur athletes to embrace the Olympic spirit. "Citius, Altius, Fortius." Swifter, Higher, Stronger.
- **The Athletes' Oath:** At the opening ceremonies, this is read by an athlete from the host country on behalf of all athletes. "In the name of all the competitors, I promise that we shall take part in these Olympic Games, respecting and abiding by the rules which govern them, committing ourselves to a sport without doping and without drugs in the true spirit of sportsmanship, for the glory of sport and the honor of our teams."
- **The Olympic Symbol:** The five colored rings linked together represent the continents of North and South America, Africa, Asia, Australia, and Europe. They also symbolize the uniting of athletes from all over the world.
- **The Olympic Flame:** This symbolizes the continuity between the ancient and modern games. The modern Olympics are opened after a torch relay, originating from the Temple of Zeus at Olympia.

Personally, I wanted Lisa on the team. She had been the most dominating player in our game. It was hard to imagine that she wasn't going to be at what might be the last Olympic softball competition ever. She knew our opponents inside and out. She had more experience than anyone. She could spot any competitor's weaknesses. I felt like we wouldn't have the same edge without her. But it wasn't in our control, and we were forced to move on.

Our preparation was different from our 2004 experience. We had a hectic pre-Olympic tour schedule that wasn't conducive to great training. We were in a different city pretty much every other day—crisscrossing the country from Ohio to Virginia to Florida to California. We had exhausting nine-hour bus rides. And we were doing all this before we even got to China.

Once we arrived in Beijing, the experience continued to be quite different. We didn't arrive early because of concerns about the air quality. Because we started competition on the second day of the Games, this time we did decide to walk in the Opening Ceremonies. I finally understood why we hadn't done it before. It was so hot and took so many hours, but I was thrilled to have the chance to experience it.

The U.S. team had to wait in the gymnastics hall for hours before marching into the stadium. President Bush came to speak to us, which instilled a sense of pride and camaraderie in Team USA—we felt like all of America was pulling for us. The walk into the stadium seemed like a kind of dreamland to me. The path was lined with local Chinese fans that had been bussed in to cheer for us, like movie extras. The Bird's Nest stadium seemed unreal. It all seemed like the Fantasyland part of Disneyland. Everything was spectacular.

One of my favorite memories is of standing in the tunnel with my teammates and the entire Team USA. Someone started the "USA, USA" cheer. It echoed off the concrete walls and gave me goosebumps.

I was sure that when we walked into the stadium we would hear an enormous roar, bigger than the Super Bowl. And when we walked out…

Nothing.

It was a huge letdown. Of course, we were the 116th country to come through. And we were one of the most disliked countries. And all the people in the stands were hot and exhausted and had been in their seats for more than ten hours.

The athletes from other countries crowded close to take pictures of our athletes—particularly Kobe Bryant. All of the U.S. athletes tried to make a barrier around him to give him some breathing room. He was swarmed everywhere he went. That was the phrase of those Olympics: Kobe, Kobe, Kobe.

Despite my internal thoughts and concerns about our team, we played great. We stormed through all our opponents. We looked like the same old dominating USA Softball team. We were doing it—we were performing in excellent USA Softball style.

But something was wrong. We weren't as confident. We didn't stick with our routine of watching video of the Japan players and going over scouting reports for the final game, I guess because we had just played them. But I was worried about deviating from our regular routines. I thrived on routine—you don't change things when they are working!

Some companies had given us some gold-accented equipment, such as cleats. I wasn't crazy about the equipment and the message it implied—that we were the presumed gold medalists. It made me nervous seeing the equipment, and I wished people would put it away until after the tournament was over. The only gold I wanted was the medal after the game was over. But some players wanted to wear it during the gold medal game. Some players were even talking about the celebration party—*before* our gold medal game! I couldn't think about anything except the game. And again these thoughts had to remain internal, Control the controllables—including yourself—we had a mission.

I was concerned we weren't functioning as one unit, but I had to let the other stuff go—I couldn't control it. It was time to put on our game faces.

The Beijing Olympics were bittersweet—in the last Olympics for softball, we didn't defend our gold medal.

In the gold medal game against Japan, Japan's offense was on fire. Japan's great pitcher Yukiko Ueno controlled us—although we got runners on base, we couldn't get them across home plate. Our game plan against Japan was to go with our lefties because Japan had so many left-handed hitters in their lineup. That was Coach's decision, and I trusted him. I couldn't let him or my teammates know that I was disappointed.

But it was hard. I really, really wanted to be in there. To just sit in the bullpen and watch our team lose was one of the hardest things I've ever done. But again a life lesson. Team always comes first—control the controllables.

I was devastated after the game. I felt like I'd let down my country. I felt like I'd let down all those women who had gone before me, the ones who had paved the way. I felt like we could have done more for our sport, for our cause. We had come to Beijing wanting to put on a show to save our sport, and we had lost. But we had to tip our hats to Japan. They are an incredible team and also had worked so very hard.

One of the things that really hurt was when people said, "Maybe this is good for the sport. Maybe it proves that the U.S. isn't as dominant. Maybe it will help softball's cause. Maybe it proves the parity in softball." When I heard IOC President Jacques Rogge say that kind of thing to Bob Costas on NBC a few days later from back in the U.S., I was so irritated.

The Olympics is supposed to be about excellence. What kind of a legacy is it to have people say that the best thing that might have happened was that we lost our last Olympic game?

I had so many thoughts in my head as I stood on the podium in Beijing. The reality that the final Olympic softball game may have just been played started to sink in. I felt I'd let down the game. I thought of all those little girls out on fields from all over the world—exactly where I had been a decade before—who had big dreams. Had I let them all down? I was crushed, especially with the future of our sport so uncertain.

On top of everything else, I missed Casey and Ace.

But in the midst of my postgame sadness came one of my favorite moments. All of the medalists—ourselves, Japan, and Australia—took softballs and wrote out 2016 on the field. We had our picture taken, arms wrapped around each, next to the message. It was a plea to bring our sport back by the 2016 Olympics. It was a moment of unity that was bigger than a gold medal loss.

> *"It's not whether you get knocked down.*
> *It's whether you get up."*
> —Vince Lombardi, Hall of Fame football coach

All of these women from different parts of the world were standing as one, coming together as one sport, working to make a difference. It was a very cool moment.

Coach Candrea called us together after the medal ceremony. We were crying. We were devastated. I know that winning a silver medal is a big accomplishment, but for many of us it felt like failure. We were the first U.S. Olympic softball team to go home without the gold medal.

Coach told us to hold our heads high and to be proud of what we had done.

"Life," he said, "is going to hand you a lot harder things than a silver medal."

Of course, he was right. He helped put things in perspective.

TOUGH LESSONS

The truth is you're going to have tough times. But those tough times can shape you into something better.

I often hear from girls who tell me they're struggling with their game or with other things in their lives. I can relate! I don't think there ever comes a time when you have it all figured out. We all battle against self-doubt every day. We all have ups and downs.

Some of my toughest times have been the most rewarding. It's where the real life lessons take place. The tough moments keep us humble and teach us discipline and desire.

The most important thing the tough times can give us is some perspective. You can't really appreciate victory without experiencing defeat.

We're working hard to grow our game and provide opportunities for the future generation. (AP Images)

One of my Olympic experiences ended with a win, the other with a loss. But my lasting memory will be of participating in something so much bigger than myself. Athletes train so hard to get there, spending so much time focusing on themselves, but then when they're at the Olympics there is a realization that the Games are really about the whole world. No matter how competitive you are, you can't help but be awed by the spirit of unity and cooperation at the Olympic Games.

While winning and losing are important, the most important things in life are faith, family, friends, and your own character.

Jennie's Tips For Dealing With a Setback

1. Acknowledge it. Tough things happen in life, but if we ignore them or pretend they didn't happen, we're probably not going to learn from them. Take a realistic look at the problem with clear eyes.

2. Focus on the good things in life. Sometimes when something bad happens it becomes such a big deal that we can't think about anything else. But don't forget all the great things in your life. Keep the setback in perspective.

3. Find something fun to do. Go to a funny movie. Hang out with good friends or family. Watch your favorite TV show. Do something that will make you smile and ease some of the negative feelings.

4. Reflect and learn. After something goes wrong, try to examine why and learn from your mistakes. Going forward, make a plan for how you will do things different the next time.

5. Stay positive! Life is full of surprises. There's a reason that people say, "The darkest hour is just before dawn." That's because sometimes when something bad happens, something fantastic is just around the corner.

Chapter 15

The Gold Medal

Twenty-five years after I first stepped on to a softball field, I stepped off.

In the summer of 2010, it seemed like the right time to step away from the game. I had never really set a retirement target date or crafted an exit strategy. I trusted my gut instinct.

Ace had spent much of his life hustling with me through airports at 5:00 AM and sleeping in hotels. Now he's older and he won't be able to keep going on the road with me when he starts school. Casey and I

Our family—before our new addition came along!

were blessed to learn, just a few months after I retired that we were going to have another son. While I'm very good at juggling, this was a time when I had to sit back, look at my life, and prioritize. When I did that, I knew it was simple: family comes first.

I was ready. But when I actually said the words, "I'm retiring," for the first time to a reporter from the Associated Press—the moment that retirement shifted from a vague idea to a concrete reality—the tears started to flow.

Even though it was time, and even though I had so many great years on the softball field as a player, it was hard for me to imagine that my time as a competitive player—an adventure that had started when I was a little kid playing T-ball—was coming to an end.

REFLECTIONS

That little kid who was told she couldn't be a championship pitcher accomplished a lot in the game of softball.

I am so grateful to all—the people in my life who supported me, to those who came before me, and to my faith—that has allowed me to have this experience as an athlete.

I was privileged to be born at the right time, into the right family, at the right place in history. I was born into a generation of girls who believed we could accomplish anything we set our minds to—and we were generally right.

I was surrounded by a loving and supportive family who believed in me as much—and at times even more—than I believed in myself. I grew up in a hotbed of youth sports, particularly softball, where there was so much opportunity to flourish and grow.

My dreams were fueled by the opportunities in front of me. By amazing collegiate programs, like my beloved University of Arizona. By the chance to play in the Olympics, which was first afforded to softball when I was 16. By the opportunity to play professionally in the National Pro Fastpitch League (NPF) with the Chicago Bandits.

> *"Aim for the moon. If you miss, you may hit a star."*
> —W. Clement Stone, philanthropist

But dreams aren't enough. It took self-belief to fulfill them. It required hard work and dedication, confidence and mental toughness to make those dreams a reality.

It takes a lot of hard work to become a champion. Those hours, weeks, and years all build up to that one moment of opportunity. When it comes, you have to seize it. You might only get one shot.

My career has given me so much: friends, health, happiness. It is the reason I met my wonderful husband and I have my beautiful children. It gave me the chance to travel the world. It even gave me the opportunity to fulfill my childhood dreams of pitching at Dodger Stadium.

I am so proud of the opportunity that is out there. Playing professionally for the Chicago Bandits in the National Pro Fastpitch League was incredible—playing against my national team teammates was a challenge every game. I'm so honored that the address of the Bandits' new home facility will be 27 Jennie Finch Way. Baseball legend Willie Mays has his own address in San Francisco (the Giants ballpark is at 24 Willie Mays Plaza). Now I have my own address. It's so very hard to believe! I still have to pinch myself.

Some of my teammates are playing professional softball in Japan. Others are coaching. I know women working as trainers, P.E. teachers, in sports media, sports marketing, and as agents. There are so many exciting career opportunities available to young women now.

I believe that everyone has his or her own special gift—a gift that can flourish regardless of circumstance, timing, or geography. Whatever your gift or talent is, if you dream big and believe in yourself, you can make it come alive. Dream and believe!

REGRETS

Of course, I regret not winning the gold medal in Beijing. My last Olympic game was a moment of frustration. A year later we defeated Japan in the Japan Cup. I pitched in that championship game, and our 2–0 victory helped erase some of the sting from Beijing.

And in 2010, we won the World Championship by beating Japan. I was honored to play first base in that game. In a way, that victory was a way of reclaiming the gold medal because without the Olympics, the World Championships are the biggest competition in our sport. We won't play another competition with the whole world until the 2014 World Championships.

Hopefully by then there will be new progress in our sport.

Of course, my biggest regret is that I couldn't do more to prevent my sport from being dropped from the Olympics. I believed that there was enough momentum to keep softball growing around the world as an Olympic sport. I believed that the rules I applied to my own life—rules about working hard, striving for excellence, and finding measurable success—would be enough to ensure that softball would remain an Olympic sport.

It wasn't. And I learned a hard lesson about the fragility of forward progress. I learned that things can be taken away in the blink of an eye. Just as life can be—my biggest life-lesson from the 2004 Olympics.

I think of all those little girls who won't get a chance to watch softball on the Olympic stage in London in 2012 or in Rio de Janeiro in 2016. I worry that the absence of such an inspirational environment might damage their dreams.

> *"I am building a fire, and every day I train, I add more fuel. At just the right moment, I light the match."*
> —Mia Hamm, soccer player

But I am determined to work to provide that environment for them because I continue to dream big myself. I dream about a day when girls will play softball in a league as big as Major League Baseball in stadiums that seat tens of thousands and are filled to capacity. I dream of traveling to other countries to teach girls around the world about the value of playing a sport, especially softball.

And I dream of one day getting our sport back on the Olympic stage.

Retirement is kind of a funny word for what I'll be doing. I won't be playing anymore, but I'll be working just as hard for this game that I love and that has given me so much.

I know now, better than ever, that it's not the end result that matters. My life didn't stop when I won the gold medal. I got up the next morning and looked forward. I asked myself, "Now what? What's the next challenge?"

Life is a constant process of striving, working, and overcoming challenges—of reaching goals and then setting new ones.

THE NEXT PHASE

In July 2010, after we won the World Cup of Softball in Oklahoma City, I set my cleats on home plate, waved to the crowd of more than 6,000 that was giving me a generous standing ovation, and walked off the field in a USA jersey for the last time.

A few weeks later, I played my last game for the Chicago Bandits after five seasons. Our final game was played in Sulphur, Louisiana—which I now call home. The NPF held its championships there, and it was an emotional and appropriate bookend to my competitive career. A God wink for sure! What were the chances that I would play my last competitive game in my husband's home town? I learned to play

"Today, you have 100 percent of your life left."
—Tom Landry, football coach

I want to always encourage girls to dream big and reach for the stars.

softball a few blocks from home in La Mirada, California. My softball career took me all over the world, but I was able to play my final game back at the place I called home.

I felt at peace with my decision to step away from competition. But it was still hard for me to believe that I wasn't going to have to throw on a regular basis and that I'll never be in a truly competitive softball game again. What I'll miss the most is traveling with my teammates, laughing on the bus, and sleeping on each other's shoulders.

Sure, I'll be on the softball field: they would have to build a pretty tall fence to keep me off! I'll continue to run camps and clinics and help coach girls. I will be actively involved in Diamond Nation in New Jersey, where I have the Jennie Finch Softball Academy. I'm sure I'll be playing exhibitions. But for me the day-in, day-out competitive world that I structured my life around is a thing of the past.

Life is a process, and I'm still working on being my best. I'm working every day on my faith, my health, my fitness, my mind, and most importantly becoming a better person, a better wife, and a better mother, striving to find my confidence and strength and find balance in my life.

Casey and I have lived a nomadic life for years, moving between whatever city he was playing in, his parents' home in Louisiana, and my parents' home in Southern California. We owned a home in Tucson but rarely had the chance to be there. We jokingly called it our "climate-controlled storage."

Now we are settling near Casey's parents' ranch in southwestern Louisiana, where we're building a place of our own. My little country boy Ace loves it—mud and fishing and four-wheel ATVs to ride around in. If feels great to have a home base again for our family. It's a place where I can retreat, recover, and refuel.

I will continue fighting for my sport in any way I can. I feel like I have so much more to give back to girls and to sports—if I can be an ambassador or a voice of support, in whatever way, that's what I will be.

And I plan to be the support system for my own children that my parents were for me. To help them reach for the stars. To make sure that they know they have what it takes to be the best they can be. To be champions.

I encourage you to be the best you can be, whether it is in the classroom, at home, or on the field. Never stop competing and striving.

Dream big. And believe!